THE SONIC WARRIOR

CHRONICLES OF A TOP GUN PIONEER

CAPTAIN KEVIN M. SMITH
U.S. NAVY, RETIRED

REDEMPTION PRESS

Published by Redemption Press, PO Box 427, Enumclaw, WA 98022.
Toll-Free (844) 2REDEEM (273-3336)

Redemption Press is honored to present this title in partnership with the author. The views expressed or implied in this work are those of the author. Redemption Press provides our imprint seal representing design excellence, creative content, and high-quality production.

The author has tried to recreate events, locales, and conversations from memories of them. In order to maintain their anonymity, in some instances the names of individuals, some identifying characteristics, and some details may have been changed, such as physical properties, occupations, and places of residence.

ISBN 13: 978-1-64645-827-1 (Paperback)
978-1-64645-500-3 (Hardback)
978-1-64645-501-0 (ePub)
978-1-64645-499-0 (Mobi)

Library of Congress Catalog Card Number: 2021923264

DEDICATION

Vice Admiral Anthony A. "Tony" Less, US Navy
Extraordinary Leader

Captain William D. "Bill" Kiper, US Navy
Air Combat Master

and

Commander Robert A. "Rob" Rivers, US Navy
Ultimate Sky Dancer

CONTRIBUTIONS

Cover Design: Jennifer Guter, Reflections Design & Print
Sizzle Reel: Kraken Video
Book Design and Edit: Jessica Stout
Cinematography: Laurie Polisky and Robert John Hadfield

TABLE OF CONTENTS

NOTE TO THE READER:

These Are Friendly Conversations

THIS IS NOT A NORMAL BOOK.

This book chronicles the life of a Sonic Warrior in a series of episodes, each one a stand-alone event, so you may find certain things are repeated. Jump around if you like—go to an episode that may involve your history as well. Some things are worthy of being repeated, such as complex-problem solving.

If you like to power read through dense material, this book is not for you. Common terms and simple sentence structure are used throughout. Technical jargon is avoided. Although sections covering combat maneuvers, critical thinking, complex-problem solving, and the three-body problem were challenging to keep simple without a loss of meaning, hopefully we have been successful.

A conversational style is utilized throughout. For example, the book begins with a Q&A. As you begin to read the book, imagine yourself sitting on your back patio around a fire pit in winter or in shirtsleeves in summer, watching the moonrise, listening to a story. So if you like a good story, read on!

We each have a story worthy of being told—this is my story.

Captain Kevin M. Smith

SONIC WARRIOR DEFINITION

A Sonic Warrior is a fighter pilot who operates near the speed of sound, neutralizing all hostile aircraft so as to achieve mission success.

Sonic Warriors operate within a four-dimensional combat arena, requiring them to employ problem-solving capabilities with ingenuity, innovation, and imagination while operating near, at, or above the speed of sound. Such capabilities are not exclusive to this elite warrior class but are available to all willing to go beyond the ordinary.

SONIC WARRIOR MOTTO

Shed Doubt and Soar!

DEFINITION OF TERMS
TYPICALLY USED IN AVIATION

aileron roll. Lateral rolling of an airplane.

air combat. Combat operations conducted in a particular airspace.

air-combat maneuvers (ACM). Complex maneuvers conducted in an airspace environment.

airborne. In the airspace environment.

airborne battle space. Air-combat arena.

airfoil. Type of wing design for an aircraft.

anchor points. Designated positions in time and space, indicating where an aircraft should be when performing a maneuver, in order to achieve optimum performance.

area rule. Diameter of the fuselage is not consistent throughout.

big-picture thinking. Maintain situation awareness of everything pertaining to the airborne environment.

bolter. To *not* catch the "wire" when landing on an aircraft carrier. As a result, the aircraft continues flying off the flight deck.

close-in air combat. Air-combat operations performed within visual range and within a five mile radius.

camber. Shape of the wing/airfoil.

catapult. Launch mechanism for aircraft aboard an aircraft carrier.

combat. Expressed as three objectives: achieve the advantage, succeed in conflict, preserve resources.

complex-problem solving. Finding solutions to problems under conditions of uncertainty. A realm of reality that is often unpredictable. See "complexity theory."

complexity. A condition which occurs when three or more agents are in play.

complexity theory. Specific body of knowledge that considers unusual behavior of complex systems.

critical thinking. Thinking that considers all aspects of a situation so as to determine the best way forward, benefiting all concerned.

decision making. Human cognitive operation intended to select the best way forward. See also operational decision making and operational risk management.

decision theory. Theoretical constructs pertaining to the decision-making process. Mathematical concepts are considered, especially probabilities.

determinism. Methodological orientation that does not embrace complexity, uncertainty, novelty.

emergent property. Occurs at the systems level that is not detected anywhere at the component level of the system.

energy management. Coordination of kinetic energy, potential energy, and propulsion (chemical) energy. Specialized training necessary.

F-8 Crusader. Lightweight supersonic fighter equipped with guns and heat-seeking missiles.

fighter. Type of combat aircraft designed to defeat other airborne targets.

fighter pilot. Air-combat warrior. Also see: Sonic Warrior, Top Gun pilot, Top Gun instructor.

fineness ratio. Streamline effect of a body moving through fluid or air, the width versus the length.

flaperons. Roll control devices located on the wings of an aircraft, distinctly different from ailerons also located on the wings.

flight deck. Upper deck of an aircraft carrier where flight operations are conducted.

G-forces (Gs). Acceleration forces experienced during turning maneuvers. Typical G-forces experienced by fighter pilots range from 4 to 8 Gs. Maximum G-forces before becoming unconscious are 4 Gs unaided, and 6-8 Gs aided.

gun pattern. Airborne engagement of simulated enemy aircraft in a mission-realistic environment. Live firing exercise.

gyroscopic. Having to do with a gyroscope, which is used to assist in stabilization.

head-up display (HUD). Cockpit display that provides critical flight information projected against transparent glass while looking through the windscreen.

information. Data that has been determined to be relevant. For more insight, research "information theory."

judgment. Ability to make sound decisions.

kinematic advisor. Includes velocity vector usually presented on the HUD.

kinematics. Motion and direction of an object.

lag maneuver. Air-combat maneuver designed to extend range from the target.

Mach 1.0. The speed at which sound travels; at 0°C/32°F, the speed of sound is 1192 km/h, 741 mph.

maneuver warfare. Formalized by Col. John Boyd USAF and considers the dynamic engagement of combat forces. Type of combat operations that emphasizes maneuverability.

maneuvers. Refers to air-combat maneuvers.

mind space. Conceptual location of that which contains the thoughts of a human.

mission critical. An event or series of events that have occurred and are threatening mission success.

mission-adaptive displays. Crew-station displays capable of automatically adapting to changing operational conditions.

nautical. Refers to nautical miles and nautical miles per hour.

never-out-list. Spare or replacement parts/components always on hand.

operational decision making. A specific decision-making process that targets the management of risk pertaining to the ability to complete the mission.

operational decision theory. Body of knowledge that considers decision making performed under increased time compression. See also operational decision making and operational risk management.

operational risk management. The process by which the risk to the operation is considered and mitigated as necessary.

probability. Level of uncertainty pertaining to how an encountered event threatens mission success.

projection. Future expectation.

rapid transience. The ability to change the state of the airplane.

reconnaissance. Gathering information on enemy forces.

roll-in. An airplane maneuver.

sidewinders. Heat-seeking missiles.

situation awareness. Necessary for mission success and included big-picture thinking. Research "Endsley's Situation Awareness Model."

sonic warfare. Combat operations conducted in the air at very high speeds, often exceeding the speed of sound.

Sonic Warrior. Air-combat specialist trained in high-speed, high-G warfare.

spoilers. Devices installed on a wing to reduce lift.

tactics manual. Strategy and tactics expressed in terms of specified maneuvers.

tactical reconnaissance. Gathering information on enemy forces utilizing airborne assets.

terrain. Ground truth.

three-body problem. Problem created when three or more objects dynamically interact with one another.

Top Gun. Intensive and advanced-training program established by the Navy to teach fighter pilots the art and skills needed to be a *successful* fighter pilot: a successful pilot with a "gun."

Top Gun instructor. Instructor pilot for Top Gun students.

Top Gun pilot. A fighter pilot who has been trained in the Top Gun training program or the methods taught in Top Gun.

turbulent flow. Related to flow dynamics, fluids, and aerodynamics.

uncertainty. Significant uncertainty prevails during any air-combat engagement.

velocity. Speed of aircraft expressed as knots. A nautical mile is used.

velocity vector. Aircraft velocity vector projected into the future.

vertical maneuver. Employed in many air-combat maneuvers. Large vertical displacements occur.

warrior. Professionally trained in the art and science of combat.

X Y Z. Coordinates of the airborne battle space.

FOREWORD

I AM STANDING ON THE FLIGHT DECK OF THE USS *MIDWAY*. THIS aircraft carrier proudly served our nation for more than forty years but now finds a home in San Diego as a museum—a great place to visit. The occasion of my visit is to do a film shoot: *The Sonic Warrior Documentary*. Our design approach is unusual in that we intend to launch *The Sonic Warrior* book and documentary as a package. This is to bring to life this compelling story in a way that brings honor to all who participated in this amazing chapter in naval aviation history. This is the story of the early Sonic Warriors and how this small group—the Top Gun pioneers—solved one of aviation's greatest challenges.

This flight deck, and others like it, represents the tip of the spear, in which protecting this great nation was the whole reason for its existence. Few nations could muster the willpower to do such a thing, but America has done it better than anyone else for nearly one hundred years.

Today we are on the flight deck of the USS *Midway* to bring honor to all who served, and all who currently serve, as part of the Naval Air Force community. In particular we honor the memory of Captain "Mo" Peele, US Navy, a longtime member of the USS Midway Museum Board of Directors. He was the commanding officer aboard the great aircraft carrier USS *Constellation* during my deployment.

The flight deck of an aircraft carrier is known as the most dangerous real estate on earth, and as such, everyone who works aboard is awarded hazardous-duty pay. Recognizing the dangers thus, prior to commencement of flight operations every daybreak, a member of the Chaplains Corps leads everyone aboard in prayer, asking the power of God to guide us and protect each one of us from harm.

Overlooking this blessed flight deck, I can see three naval aircraft that feature prominently in *The Sonic Warrior* book and film documentary: the F-4 Phantom II, the F-8 Crusader, and the F-14 Tomcat II. All three aircraft were seriously supersonic. The Sonic Warriors within these communities worked together to solve the challenge of improving the close-in-air-combat performance of our frontline fighter forces.

Like the USS *Midway* but larger, the USS *Constellation* was the operational home of the first forward-deployed Top Gun unit. This unit, which I commanded, provided advanced close-in-air-combat experience for the F-14 squadrons—along with other squadrons as well—during our Pacific deployment. In the process we made aviation history. This achievement would not have been possible without Captain Peele's leadership aboard the USS *Constellation*. Indeed, he provided key resources for the squadron that I was commanding to enable us to increase our operational tempo by more than 25 percent, ensuring overall mission success.

Some of the ideas we developed operating supersonic aircraft from a flight deck such as this have applications in other domains as well. One such idea relates to the consideration of *time* when performing a decision-making activity during the course of a complex military operation. The *time* valuation took a while to be acceptable, but I am happy to announce that this year it is now officially recognized as a key component within the body of knowledge known as "decision theory."

The Sonic Warrior: Chronicles of a Top Gun Pioneer has piqued your interest if you are reading this foreword. Welcome! Keep in mind that these are stories that can be read in any order, although they are roughly arranged chronologically.

The companion film *The Sonic Warrior Documentary* is planned to show at several film festivals throughout the United States. Check out our website for more details at thesonicwarrior.com.

—Captain Kevin M. Smith, US Navy (Ret.)
USS *Midway* Flight Deck, May 4, 2021
San Diego, California

Flight Lieutenant John Gillespie Magee Jr.
(1922–1941)

HIGH FLIGHT

By Flight Lieutenant John Magee Jr., Royal Canadian Air Force

Oh, I have slipped the surly bonds of earth.
And danced the skies on laughter-silvered wings:
Sunward I've climbed and joined the tumbling mirth of sun-split clouds—
And done a hundred things you have never dreamed of—
wheeled and soared and swung high in the sunlit silence.
Hovering there I've chased the shouting wind along
and flung my eager craft through footless halls of air . . .

Up, up the long delirious burning blue
I've topped the wind-swept heights with easy grace,
where never lark, or even eagle, flew—
and while with silent, lifting mind I've trod
the high untrespassed sanctity of space,
put out my hand and touched the face of God.

A Supermarine Spitfire Mk. Vb, RF-D, flown by pilot Jan Zumbach (1915–1986) of the 303 Kosciuszko Polish Fighter Squadron of the Royal Air Force (RAF), World War II, circa 1943. The aircraft bears Zumbach's distinctive Donald Duck symbol.

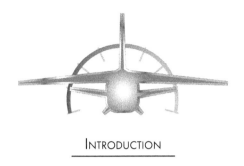

THE WONDER OF FLIGHT

THERE IS A LINE IN THE VERY FAMOUS POEM WRITTEN BY JOHN MAGEE Jr. and it goes, "Oh, I have slipped surly bonds of earth, and danced the skies on laughter-silvered wings." He was expressing this wonder, this magical thing that we have developed, that we have somewhat perfected—the magic and wonder of flight. Humans could finally take to the air and soar and climb and dive and do all kinds of wonderful things. They could travel over great distances at speeds that were unheard of a few years ago—speeds that were quite extraordinary. And then we were able to conduct many different kinds of flight operations on a regular basis—privately, commercially, and militarily.

We were able to break the speed of sound as well. That was really quite extraordinary. It was not known that we could do such a thing. We didn't know a whole lot, but we decided that we were going to do it anyway. We had this vision—that humans could not only achieve flight, but break the sound barrier as well. It was extraordinarily difficult to do and yet we did, in 1947.

With this newfound knowledge, confidence, extraordinary level of bravery, and the desire to explore the unknown, we were able to design, build, and operate airplanes that could easily travel at speeds at and above the speed of sound and do all kinds of amazing things. Most of these started out as military aircraft, but there were some attempts at commercial aircraft. As I write this, there is a newfound enthusiasm and emphasis on supersonic flight. We have all kinds of projects underway to bring within the sphere of commercial aviation—aircraft that are capable of operating efficiently and effectively at speeds above the speed of sound. Supersonic flight is again front and center as we move into the twenty-second century.

A Sonic Warrior is defined as a fighter pilot, one who conducts combat operations near, at, or beyond the speed of sound. This book chronicles the time I spent in the earlier years of supersonic flight—the time that I spent flying aircraft that were capable of achieving these extraordinary levels of speed. These aircraft were military, which were at that time the only ones available and capable of achieving such speeds. I flew two supersonic-capable airplanes, the F-11 Tiger and F-8 Crusader. The F-11 Tiger's top speed was about Mach 1.2 at a relatively high altitude, between 30,000 and 40,000 feet. (Typically, it's 35,000 feet, but it varies based upon the condition you find yourself operating in.) The F-8 Crusader was, at one time, the fastest aircraft in the world. Its speeds were quite extraordinary. It was clocked officially at Mach 1.6, which is about 1,025 miles per hour. (For reference, Mach 1.0 equals the speed at which sound travels.) It's the first aircraft to break the 1,000-miles-an-hour barrier. Mach 1.6 was really quite an achievement. No other airplane had even come close to achieving that speed. That speed proved to be decisive in combat engagements. This aircraft become known as the "MiG Master" as a result of its extraordinary performance in the Vietnam War. It was a frontline air defense fighter for many years, primarily operating from smaller aircraft carriers. Many of the following fighter airplanes were not so capable. Eventually, models of the airplane unofficially exceeded Mach 1.8, getting pretty close to Mach 1.9. That was an amazing achievement not that well recognized previously. But here we're recognizing the extraordinary capability of such an airplane.

Why was it necessary to achieve such speeds? It was necessary for a number of reasons. This speed advantage was proven to be decisive during World War II when they introduced the P-51 Mustang for bomber escort. The speed advantage of that airplane over its competitors or over the enemy aircrafts' capabilities was about 100 knots, and that proved to be really quite decisive. With that capability you can move across the airborne battlespace quicker, outrun your enemy, hide behind clouds and pounce upon the enemy quicker than the enemy can attack you, or avoid enemy contact altogether. With higher speed comes the need for higher ability to achieve more effective maneuvers. Your maneuver profile changes with the higher speeds. For example, you can exploit the vertical much better the more speed that you have. So as a weapons system, with respect to the national defense of the United States of America, this great country of ours, speed was an extremely important part of that picture strategically as well as tactically.

The extraordinary F-8 Crusader was feared by our enemies during the Cold War. It was honored and highly respected by all aviators who were flying during that period of time. It was so extraordinary that the test of any combat-capable fighter was, "How well does it perform against the F-8 Crusader?" That was the ultimate test. You could say what you wanted about your favorite aircraft, but if it didn't have that engagement record, then it was not considered to be worthy until we could determine realistically and factually how well it performed against what aviators at the time considered the finest fighter that was ever designed.

My story is primarily about my time as an F-8 Crusader fighter pilot and all the various things that I and my fellow squadron pilots did during this time in aviation. We are documenting it here for many reasons. Some of them are historical, and some are lessons learned that we should never forget. What brought us success needs to be clearly identified so we can maintain our progress in this domain of the Sonic Warrior and sonic warfare. The fighter pilot community has gone through many iterations. The major challenges that we faced and were able to overcome occurred during this era—roughly the 1960s through the 1980s, about thirty years' worth of time. During that time, we learned a lot of things. There were things that were unexpected, and there were certain aspects of aerial combat that were not as accurate as we thought. There were a lot of things that we learned and a lot of new ideas that entered into this particular arena of sonic warfare.

Just to point out a few, it was pretty obvious that aircraft that could operate in the vicinity of 450 to 500 knots—converging on Mach 1.0—were much more difficult to defeat. They are very difficult to locate. To keep these aircraft in some kind of a view, whether with the naked eye or with the help of an electronic system, is extremely difficult. Speed, maneuverability, and agility were the three legs of the performance triad. However, agility was not recognized as important as it should have been. This major defect in our thinking and design approach was pointed out by Colonel John Boyd, United States Air Force. He is considered one of the best fighter pilot minds ever to have existed. As an Air Force fighter pilot, he contributed immensely to the knowledge base that helped us as we struggled with many issues.

The key to our progress was understanding the Human-Machine System.

There is a human side to this arena that we call the Sonic Warrior. How did humans think while traveling at these high speeds, maneuvering, and experiencing very high G loads? How did humans perform? How did they deal with these extremely difficult issues, circumstances, and this highly complex environment? Ultimately the question is, "How do humans perform in a complex, time-compressed environment?" How do they do that? How should we train humans to perform well in a highly complex, time-compressed environment in which high G-forces are the order of the day? How should we train them to perform well? How should we ensure that they maintain proficiency in this highly dynamic environment, in which constantly practicing all of these skill sets is a must? How do we deal with that? What lessons do we need to learn about the human side of this equation? The airplanes were marvelous inventions from a physical standpoint, but from a cognitive standpoint, what else was needed?

We needed to match the physical performance of the airplane with the cognitive performance of the human. That match is one of the things I address in this book. I address the human side—the magnificence of the human spirit and the human ability to perform in such stressful and trying environments. The human spirit can soar above the fray, can keep its wits about it when things seem to be completely falling apart, can overcome adversity, and can achieve resilience when it seems impossible to do so. How do humans do that? What are the lessons learned? What is the body of knowledge with respect to the human aspect in this environment of sonic warfare? How do we select people for this job and establish highly effective training programs and instructional systems? Do we have a concerted effort underway that systematically addresses itself to optimizing human performance in the world of sonic warfare?

One of the things that I would like readers to take away from this book is the final notion of optimizing human performance when the environment is complex, time compressed, and very stressful. That is a profoundly important challenge as we consider aviation as an arena in which new ideas, concepts, inventions, and innovations are always welcome and encouraged—not only for aircraft but also for the human cognitive system. How can we improve it, how can we enhance it, and how can we optimize it? Here we get into all kinds of aspects of preparing the human mind, establishing the protocols and the behaviors, and developing human cognitive capabilities for ongoing performance. How can we deal with that in a coherent way? How do we match the human with the machine? How can we enhance human learning along with machine learning, and how can we match them up even better in future aerospace systems? These are our challenges as we go forward. This book, along with my other efforts, has helped clarify these issues.

Captain Kevin M. Smith, US Navy
Portrait as squadron commander operating aboard the USS *Constellation*.

CAPTAIN KEVIN SMITH DISCUSSES THE SONIC WARRIOR

A Video Interview with Captain Kevin Smith and His Wife, Sue Smith

SUE: HELLO, I'M HERE WITH CAPTAIN KEVIN SMITH. I'M SUE SMITH, his wife. We're going to discuss his work and some of his significant career milestones. We're inviting everyone to listen in, though we would like to tell our radio audience that the full video and audio of this conversation will be available on Kevin's radio show website www.throttleupradio.com and his YouTube channel *The Sonic Warrior*. So, Kevin, tell everyone why you wanted to have this conversation and make this book and video.

Kevin: Okay, good question. First of all, I'm glad to be here. And thank you for being here as well, helping out, and keeping me on track. I think probably two reasons. Number one is that I see a continuing, heightened—or new, perhaps, not just continuing—interest in this country in two areas. One of them is the recognition of the need for leadership, the need for effective leaders, leaders that can help us through difficult times. The second reason is the renewed interest in the most recent *Top Gun* movie. The *Top Gun* movie trailer has been released to rave reviews. It's gone viral online—I think in two days it had more than twenty million hits. And I was involved in that Top Gun initiative. So probably it's time for me to talk about my involvement in how the Top Gun program propelled and supported and helped other interests and other things that came after it. Some of it is the work that I have done and the work of others. I'm within that group of people who were involved and responsible for that initiative being successful and how we could use and leverage that to help other programs.

Sue: Will you tell us a little bit about the start of your Navy career?

Kevin: Yes. I guess you could say that I started out as a Sonic Warrior. And what does that mean? I was going through the Naval Air Academy as a student naval aviator. I was learning to fly Navy airplanes. I eventually got into the supersonic pipeline. I'm not exactly sure how I wound up there. It wasn't available to everyone. But nevertheless, I was selected to go through the supersonic pipeline. One of the airplanes that they used for the supersonic training was the F-11 Tiger. And you know, that was the first supersonic airplane that was ever built. And I got to fly that in various modes and various mission-realistic training scenarios. So I guess you're going to ask me what it was like to fly supersonic airplanes?

Sue: Yes, exactly.

Kevin: I would say that it was certainly a thrill a minute, but it was also challenging. The bottom line is that I thoroughly enjoyed it. These planes are highly maneuverable—very fast and just a joy to ride. Ride like you would ride a motorcycle or ride like a fast horse. So we were in that mode of thinking. But of course it was quite challenging too. One of the challenges we had—we had to figure out how to actually perform aerial combat at sonic speeds. It'd never been done before. So we were working in that area. A lot of it was trial and error. There wasn't much in the way of corporate knowledge or best practices. We were basically on the ground floor trying to figure it out as best we could.

Sue: How does the "gunsight HUD" figure into those challenges?

Kevin: Yeah, that was probably one of the biggest challenges we had. Now the HUD, head-up display, was invented during World War II for the propeller-driven fighters of that day. But then when we got into the jet era, and we got into the supersonic era, the head-up display was modified to become more dynamic. It was a gyro-stabilized gunsight, so it had gyroscopic information; it wasn't just fixed. The problem, though, was this: the airplane-flying characteristics when it goes supersonic were entirely different. So it was like flying two different airplanes in the same fuselage. Now flying characteristics were different for lots of reasons. A lot of them are physics or science—stuff like that. The fact remains that it became a different airplane characteristically, and the gyro-stabilized head-up display wasn't smart enough at the time to understand that. So the supersonic regime was such that whatever information we had to aim our guns wasn't effective.

Sue: Now this was during your training you were running into these issues?

Kevin: Right. I realized very quickly that you had to disregard the information, and you had to be able to anticipate what the airplane was going to do before it actually did something in the supersonic regime. And the problem was in the air-combat engagement there was a place in the envelope where you went from supersonic flight to subsonic flight because you were pulling a lot of Gs. And that transition from supersonic regime to subsonic regime produced all kinds of control difficulties. And you actually had to be able to anticipate that before it actually happened. If you didn't anticipate that, the plane would stall, you would spin out, and you would be in serious trouble.

Sue: Now were you using the F-11 Tiger at this point, or are you starting to talk about your career in the F-8 Crusader?

Kevin: That was the F-11 Tiger; that was the first supersonic airplane that I flew. Then I quickly transitioned into the F-8 Crusader, which was a remarkable airplane. It stayed in the fleet operation for a very long period of time. It was very advanced. I loved it, by the way. It was carrier-based, as it turns out. And it was the first airplane to exceed 1,000 miles per hour. Airplanes I was flying at the time were brand new and were delightful and very responsive and extremely high-performance airplanes.

Sue: What time frame was this? What year?

Kevin: This was mid-1960s when I started flying the supersonic Crusader. I'm kind of surprised that a lot of people don't understand the history of aviation, but nevertheless, I think it has an amazing story to tell, the airplane. And my involvement is important as well. The F-8 Crusader was the only airplane that was awarded the Collier Trophy and the Thompson Trophy.

Sue: So you're going to explain what those awards meant, please?

Kevin: Those awards basically for lots of reasons were awarded to that airplane and the design team because it set a number of speed records. Some of those speed records have never been duplicated. To give an example, one of the things that was extremely important during that period of time was to be able to launch from an airport or an aircraft carrier and be able to climb at an extremely rapid rate to intercept bombers. And that was one of our major jobs as fighter pilots. The airplane could actually go from zero airspeed to Mach 1.0 at 35,000 feet in under five minutes.

Sue: Sounds fast!

Kevin: It's five minutes. You can be intercepting an enemy bomber in five minutes.

Sue: Off the carrier.

Kevin: Off the carrier, yes.

Sue: Amazing.

Kevin: It was really quite remarkable. We used to have this maneuver. This is kind of fun. And I used to love to do it. At that particular point in time when you read 35,000 feet, the nose of the airplane was so high it was actually difficult and uncomfortable to push it over because you would go into zero Gs and things would fly all over the cockpit and you would feel kind of funny and stuff like that, so we used to do what we call a burner roll. We would actually do an aileron roll and come back to a level flight. That was fun. I used to love to do that.

The next big story was the F-8. That airplane had conventional weapons for a fighter, which were guns, which were around for a long time—actually since World War I. Fighter airplanes had guns, and the F-8 Crusader had guns as well. They were actually pretty big guns. They were 20-millimeter cannons, so they were not machine guns. Fifty calibers were machine guns. But the 20-millimeters were considered cannons. So we had four 20-millimeter cannons. But also we carried the first-generation missiles that were called sidewinders. They were heat-seeking missiles. And that made it a formidable weapons system. It was quite well equipped; it was highly respected in combat—very effective in combat.

Sue: So now you were involved with Top Gun—the very beginnings of Top Gun. Why don't you tell the folks about that?

Kevin: Yeah, I guess you could say that was the beginning of my journey, although my journey started training as a supersonic warrior, going through the first supersonic era. But then Top Gun popped up on the radar, so to speak, and that was because of two reasons. Number one: the combat effectiveness of US Air Forces (the Naval Air Forces and United States Air Force)—combat effectiveness of the tactical fighter program during Vietnam in 1968 was not very good—there was very poor performance particularly in the F-4 community. Then a rather critical thing happened. We could say that it was a crisis that had occurred because it was completely unexpected. We thought that these brand-new F-4 airplanes were appropriate for the combat conditions encountered. They were actually good airplanes and good pilots, but the pilots were not properly trained for the environment, and the airplane wasn't particularly equipped to handle the environment we were putting the airplane in. And things went downhill very rapidly performance-wise. And so a lot of people hit the panic button. There were some major studies done very quickly. One famous study was called the *Ault Report*. That was probably the most thorough examination of the problem and the problem space. I think this is probably more important than anything else—and I think that this is the lesson for all of us—the solution came from the grassroots level. It was a grassroots initiative.

Sue: From the line pilots, is that what you're saying?

Kevin: The active pilot community. Not the bureaucracy, not the headquarters and all that snuff. Notwithstanding, I'm not suggesting that the headquarters were not good people. They were and they are. They are good, solid officers and very capable. But the fact remains that the fighter pilot who was there saw things that were not clearly visible to anybody else because it was a very difficult problem to deal with. And the environment was extremely complex. Remember that back then we were still learning about supersonic airplanes and energy management that we didn't know. There is no energy management dial in the airplane. There is no energy management display in the airplane. But we had to understand what our energy was, not only in the present time but also at some point in the future. So I like to think of it as this: we had to be able to figure out a future situation from a set of current events. Now that's extremely hard to do cognitively. It can be done, but it can only be done through proper training. You have to be formally trained in order to do that.

Sue: And you're talking about the future events that the combat pilot has in his role as a combat pilot. You're talking about those scenarios where he has to be able to anticipate what is happening.

Kevin: Absolutely right. And be correct about it, and be accurate, right? So everything in the cockpit is in the here and now. We had to be able to take that and do what I call "mental projection." We had to be able to figure out accurately where the enemy airplane was *going to be*, not only where it is now. But where it was going to be based upon our understanding of the performance characteristics of our plane and the enemy's airplane. I used to teach this. I would tell my students that you not only have to fly your airplane, but you have to fly the enemy airplane as well. You have to fly both airplanes simultaneously. And you have to be able to anticipate not only where your airplane can be but where the other airplane will be. So that was extremely important. That was not known up to this point. The other thing was that missile technology—missiles were new—was a new thing that humans had just come up with. The original missile was called the sidewinder, which was actually invented and built by the Naval Air Weapons Center China Lake. You and I have been to China Lake, and we have done some museum speaking engagements there at their museum. The Naval Air Weapons Center China Lake invented the sidewinder. That happened to be a good weapons system but short range.

Now we wanted to go longer range, so we put longer range missiles on the Phantom, but we didn't give it any guns since we thought that the Phantom was going to deal with long-range intercepts. Because the missiles were going to be able to shoot down the enemy airplane before they got into a close-in combat situation, we thought that was going to be good enough. That turned out to be wrong. That was a wrong assumption. And so the Phantom was faced with what we call "close-in-air combat," or another term that is used is "dogfight." The Phantom was faced with close-in-air combat. Crews didn't know how to do that because they weren't trained. I was asked to help train the crews in close-in-air combat before they went to Vietnam. Now up to this point they were learning on the job once they got to the combat zone, which turned out to be a rather poor solution to a very difficult problem. It wasn't very effective. So the idea was, "That doesn't make any sense. Let's actually prepare them for close-in-air combat before they have to deploy to a combat zone." My job—I may have been the first pilot assigned to this—and this was grassroots by the way. Because the Phantom community—when I was stationed at Oceana, and you were there with me, remember that? The Phantom community—they were screaming for training, and they came to my squadron, and we were flying the F-8 Crusader, and our airplane almost identically matched the enemy airplane in performance, the MiG-21. So that grassroots effort basically generated this Top Gun initiative. I may have been the first pilot assigned to that role. And my job was to train the Phantom crews to perform well and succeed in a close-in-air combat situation.

Sue: And that effort expanded into working with the F-14 community as well, right?

Kevin: Yes, exactly right. And I would call that, in terms of my career milestone, Top Gun II. There is actually a second *Top Gun* movie, but this is my actual Top Gun II experience. So the second phase of my Top Gun work was working with the F-14. Now at that time the F-14 was the Navy's brand-new frontline fighter, brand-spanking-new, fifty million dollars, right out of the factory. And again, the grassroots initiative took over, and it became quite apparent that this airplane, while it had pretty good stand-off capabilities for a modern fighter, didn't have a lot of information in the cockpit that could help you in close-in-air combat. So this whole idea of trajectory and energy management, all that stuff, was pretty much left up to the human operator or the ingenuity, innovation, and creativity of the human. Because the machine was really not very much help. So the F-14 community that was part of Air Wing 9—I was part of Air Wing 9 as well—they went to the air wing commander who happened to be Captain Tony Less, who, I think, you've met.

Sue: Right, yes.

Kevin: You know Tony. Tony eventually made it to Vice Admiral. He was a very highly regarded Navy pilot and naval aviator. And he was the air wing commander. I was the squadron commander right under him. He and I got together, and we got this idea that we were going to train the F-14 air crews in close-in-air combat while on deployment. It was a brand-new idea. Now of course, as you can imagine, a lot of people said it couldn't be done. So that leads me to Top Gun III. Top Gun III was actually the first *deployed* Top Gun unit. I was the commander of the first deployed Top Gun unit because no one had been able to figure out how to take the Top Gun training program, the training curriculum, and export it to an aircraft carrier. So that was a brand-new idea, way outside the box. Training crews in close-in-air combat was an important job that had to be done because they were not particularly proficient in that area. So we were trying to optimize human performance when humans have to perform complex activities. That's what we were trying to do. It's not easy. It has to be done. We really didn't have any choice. You can't just give up and say, "I give up," and go home when you are on deployment on a carrier. You're the tip of the spear. So we had no choice but to do the best that we possibly could. And so I was the squadron commander of the initiative of that first deployed Top Gun unit, and as it turns out, we were able to provide meaningful close-in-air combat training for the F-14 community in the Pacific fleet at that time.

Sue: And you won an award for your efforts, right?

Kevin: Yes, yes, I did. A citation and a medal, so I was glad and a bit humbled about it. Certainly, I was grateful that it was recognized. It was in fact quite a difficult challenge as it turns out. There're a lot of moving pieces when you try to take this stuff on a carrier. There're a lot of moving parts. There are a lot of things that could go wrong. Not the least of which you could have some serious accidents.

Sue: So what are the things from these experiences as squadron commander, the issues with combat training—what did you learn from this that you carried forward to your other career, your career outside of the Navy?

Kevin: Well, the first thing that comes to mind is that everything that we thought we knew about performing well in a dynamic, fluid, complex environment like aerial combat turned out to be wrong. And there are lots of reasons for that. I'm not talking about people not doing the best they could—they all were. But there are a lot of misconceptions about what could optimize human performance. I'll give you an example. I used to take new fighter pilots out and train them in all of these complex combat maneuvers. I quickly learned that before I got into any of the specifics of maneuver warfare, I had to address two things right up front. The first thing I had to address was I had to break through the fear barrier. I had to prove to these young pilots that the airplane was not going to kill them, that I was not going to kill them in my close-in-combat maneuvers, and they should not be afraid. The second thing I had to do was make sure that they had enough self-confidence that I could actually train them in these complex maneuvers. Both of those things are nontechnical but vital. If I couldn't do that, I would fail in my job as a Top Gun instructor.

Sue: So do you want to tell us about the F-22 project?

Kevin: Yeah, so whatever I learned, experienced, and was able to deal with effectively in the area of air combat and the Top Gun initiative that I was involved with for a long period of time, I took with me when I got involved with the F-22 project. The F-22 project was the first fifth-generation fighter that we built as a nation—first fifth-generation fighter in the world as it turns out. And there was a considerable amount of concern because we were going from a crew of two back to a crew of one. Now of course the F-8 Crusader was a crew-of-one airplane, single-piloted airplane. But the F-4 and the F-14 were a pilot and the naval flight officer in the back who was the weapons-systems operator, so it was a crew of two. Now we were going back to a single crew member in the F-22, and that was a very difficult thing because we had to figure out how to take all of this high technology and package it in a way that a single pilot could operate it effectively. That was a huge challenge for the industry, a huge challenge for the Department of Defense, and a huge challenge for the research community. We had a lot of research involvement. For example, there was a component of the program that was being funded by DARPA. The Defense Advance Research Project Agency was involved in this initial design effort. So I was brought in to help with the cockpit environment because it had to be designed in a way to accommodate a single crew member.

Sue: This was after your active-duty days, correct?

Kevin: Right. Yes, I had retired from the Navy, and I was asked by Lockheed to come in and help them out with the design of the crew station for the F-22.

Sue: Right. And you worked on design specs, or . . .

Kevin: That's a really interesting question because when I first went in there, everybody thought that we were going to deal with whatever information was being presented on the flight displays. We call them glass displays or glass cockpits. These were multi-function displays so you could put up a lot of information. So everybody thought that I was going to be dealing with the display features. As it turns out, I did deal with some of the display features, but I quickly realized that there was something else that needed to be done before you actually designed the display features. And that was to consider very carefully, "What is your design model by which you are able to create these display features that are agile and adaptable?" So in complex language here, the design team that I was on was trying to figure out this: "How do you actually enable or make the cockpit systems agile and adaptive?" The challenge was, "How you do build a complex, adaptive system?" Simple, right? It's a simple phrase, but it's extremely difficult to do because the system has to know something that current systems don't. The system has to be able to recognize events before the pilot tells it to. The system has to be working with the flight crew and not after the flight crew has figured things out. The system has to be helping. So the complex, adaptive systems were the challenge. The problem was to figure out the design. The design model we were using was created during the analog era, and it didn't work for digital systems. It didn't work.

Sue: So you discovered some new models for this, right?

Kevin: Well, we had to. We had no choice but to come up with a different design model. The current design model, which was technology-driven, didn't work. It simply didn't work. It was bottom-up technology engineering. It worked great for analog systems, but for digital systems it didn't work. And the other thing that we were asked to do was extremely important and probably the most important point. I wish I'd made it sooner. We made the first airplane that I know of, if you understand the terms here. I'm trying to make them simple—it was the first digital airplane. We have this digital environment, we are living in a digital world now, and all these systems can actually communicate with one another.

Sue: And what airplane was that? The F-22?

Kevin: It was the F-22 Fighter. So it was the first digital airplane, the first data bus airplane, which means it had a 1552 data bus, which basically meant the systems could communicate with one another. The problem was if you can do that, then how do you integrate at a higher level? How do you create a higher-order-reasoning capability within a man-machine system? Extremely important to do such a thing. That design model didn't exist. And we had to create it.

Sue: And who was "we"?

Kevin: The design team I was on. It was actually a gang of five. We were the mavericks. We were the outliers. We were considered to be crazy. We were the gang of five. We said, "No, you need a new design model." And so we came up with a new design model. We didn't just say you needed one—we actually created a new design model, which we presented at the Digital Avionics Systems Conference at the time in San Jose. We presented that.

Sue: So on to your next big career challenge. What would you say that was?

Kevin: Well, the next big career challenge was pilot training. So after I finished my work on the F-22 and we did the best we could, we came up with some really good system concepts. And we went on and designed a brand-new Airline Pilot Training System employing the lessons learned from the last thirty years. I think it probably could've been better, but that's just the nature of the world. The next big challenge was the 3:00 a.m. phone call. You've probably heard of that. This actually didn't occur quite this way, but close enough. So I get this emergency phone call at 3:00 a.m., and this guy calls me up, a friend of mine, and says, "When can you get to the training center of this airline because all hell has broken loose?" And I said, "I don't know, when do you need me?" and he says, "Yesterday." And I say, "Well, that's pretty quick. What's going on?" And he says, "Well, we're in pretty serious trouble training-wise." So I go up there, and they offer me this management position. You know how I am, right? I accept this management position.

Sue: Anxious to help out.

Kevin: Anxious to help out. So I accepted the management position and got involved in redesigning airline pilot training. Now I thought that I was going to be involved with redesigning airline pilot training for this airline. No, not true. The job was to redesign air pilot training for all airlines. So that meant that I was a member of a federal task force, sponsored by the federal government, jointly sponsored by the Air Transport Association. So my job was to redesign airline pilot training for all US carriers. And you're probably going to ask me, "How did that work out?"

Sue: Kevin, how did that work out?

Kevin: Quite successfully by the way. All the airlines are now using that training model. All of them. Every single one. Most European airlines are also using the training model, same one. What was the motivation? What generated this industry-wide initiative? It was motivated by rising accident rates that were being experienced in the airline industry back in approximately 1987. It was motivated by a lot of concern within the industry, in the federal agencies, and within Congress. They put together a blue-ribbon task force under the Reagan administration, and the task force came up with a bunch of ideas, and one of the ideas was the current airline pilot training program was kind of frozen in time. It was difficult to modify it, so we needed a new way to upgrade pilot training. So Congress allowed us the flexibility to do that. And it eventually became known as Advanced Qualification Program initiative, or AQP. I was a member of the AQP working group, federally sponsored, and also chairman of the Training Integration Taskforce. So I was at a very high level, and my job was to figure out how to upgrade airline pilot training and bring it up to the current time frame in terms of airplane and equipment but also in our understanding of human performance from a psychological standpoint, not just a textual standpoint. So two things emerged from this—very significant. These were huge breakthroughs in thinking. We moved away from an almost exclusive focus on technology. We said, "Technology has its place, but it is not the focal point." The focal point is the human and the ability of the human to solve complex problems. The human is supported by technology; the human is supported by psychology. But the human's ability to understand and solve complex problems very quickly and effectively—that was the focal point. And so we moved everything to the human and the human cognitive system. People don't quite understand what that means. I thought it'd be fairly straightforward. But the human possesses a cognitive system that is capable of doing things that otherwise cannot be done. The human has a marvelous system. It is innovative, it is creative, it is adaptive, and it is agile. It has all of those characteristics. The most important thing is that it can solve problems that are difficult to solve. It has great problem-solving capabilities. And so we focus on the human, we took the human as the centerpiece, and we worked on the human side; we brought in all kinds of things, and we also realized that the human thinks about systems and thinks about the mission. The human does not do very well on the lower-level stuff.

Sue: So now this is where your work on mission-adaptive displays fits in?

Kevin: Correct, yes. So what we discovered was if you really want to improve performance, no matter what you're doing, no matter what industry you're in, it doesn't matter whether or not you're a seasoned professional, or you're a beginner, or you're a graduate student—it doesn't matter. What we discovered was that in order to improve performance, if you are operating with sophisticated equipment, you have to be able to get the equipment to give you certain things at the right time to help your performance. That's called a performance aid. Now the beauty of modern technology is that we can change display features in nanoseconds, right?

Sue: Well, almost.

Kevin: Almost, right? Remember in the analog era the display was given, right? It was frozen. But no longer. We can change the display features very, very quickly in the digital era, so why don't we get the display features smart enough to get the human needs at that particular time? It's called a performance aid, a real-time performance aid. Or another term that I use is "mission-ready performance aids."

Sue: And so one of your contributions to your field of aviation is your textbook on mission-adaptive display technologies, where you have made this sort of approach available to the general public.

Kevin: Yes. Exactly right, yes. So I had an opportunity to write this textbook. It's a research-essentials book, published by IGI Global, a large publishing house for technical material. And I was honored to write it. But yes, it's a textbook that we both worked on putting together, but it is a textbook that deals with mission-adaptive displays. Another general term that we use is "mission-ready adaptive systems." The title of the book is *Mission Adaptive Display Technologies and Operational Decision Making in Aviation*. That is a mouthful. But that pretty well describes what the textbook is all about. Now what it says is, "Okay, if we are able to technically get the displays to modify themselves with a particular trigger, why don't we do it?" and you can say, "Well, Kevin, are the triggers there in the airplane already, or do you have to build the triggers and all of that stuff?" The answer is, no, the triggers are already there, we just have to recognize the triggers that are there. And then once we have the trigger, it can actually produce a display feature that would be considered to be a performance aid to help the flight crews better perform this complex activity. The answer is yes, you can do that technically, but why don't we do it? Well, we don't do it. It's not because we don't have the technical capability to do that—we do. We don't have the design model that informs that process.

Sue: And you have another book that we're all proud of, your *Critical Thinking Essentials*. So why don't you tell everyone about that?

Kevin: Yes, I would be glad to do that. That's a good lead-in. *Critical Thinking Essentials*. I started to write other books as well, and I wrote a number of short books. I started to do author events, also called book-signing events, at bookstores across the country. And so lots of them, you know, are private ma-and-pa bookstores all the way up to Barnes & Noble—and you've been with me on a number of those events. And I got talking to people, and I learned from the people I met. It was a wonderful experience because you never know who is going to walk in through the door of a bookstore: a random sample of Americans. And I talked to all of them, and I asked them about themselves, and they'd tell me about themselves or what they do or what they have done and what is their interest. Well, they're interest was, above everything else: "I want to learn how to think critically, and I want to learn how to do that better."

Sue: Well, we're hearing a lot about that from a lot of different sources these days—about the importance of critical-thinking courses in the colleges. And I would say you have been in the forefront of this activity, this pursuit.

Kevin: Yes, I mean, you and I went to Europe recently; we had a speaking engagement there in Brussels. Well, I'll give you an example to prove this point, all right? The World Economic Forum meets in Davos, Switzerland, every year, and they put out a report. So the latest *Future of Jobs* report put out by the World Economic Forum says that critical thinking and complex-problem solving are the number one sought-after skills in the global job market and also the most difficult to fill. I rest my case. What else can I say? In fact, you and I just came back from an author event at Barnes & Noble in Idaho Falls. It was a big two-day event. And we learned once again that people are clamoring for more stuff on critical thinking. Now what I didn't want to do—I didn't just want to hand them this dense book with lots and lots of words and be difficult to get through and that was going to sit on their shelf or coffee table, and they would thumb through it and pretty much forget it. I was not willing to do that. There are lots of books like that. There are. I wanted to do something different, something out of the box. And I thought to myself, "What do they need?" Well, they need something that is easily accessible and effective, that's what they need. Something you can get into quickly and get on with your job, your work, your life, and then pick it up again whenever you have the need for it. The way I like to explain it, and I do it with everyone I meet: This handbook is part of your "go bag." Your go bag in the military—you always had one packed because you never knew when you were going to get called up and fly to the ends of the world to solve a crisis. But the go bag is when your organization or personally you have a crisis, and you have to go someplace to solve it—that's part of your go bag. That sits right next to your shaving/cosmetic kit. You take it with you.

Sue: The *Critical Thinking Essentials Handbook*?

Kevin: You take that with you when you go out to solve a critical problem. And it takes you through the steps that you need to take. One of the biggest problems we have is we tend to jump ahead without spending some quality time on defining the problem. What is the problem for which you seek a solution? A famous quote from Einstein, and I don't actually know if this is true, but I use it because it sounds good, and I think it is true. Somebody asked Einstein this hypothetical question. They said, "If you have an hour to figure out how to save the world from annihilation, what would you do? How would you spend your hour?" And he said, "I would spend fifty-five minutes of that hour trying to figure out the problem. And the rest is simple mathematics." That was his answer.

Sue: Well, mathematics right now is telling us that it is time to close our discussion.

Kevin: Really?

Sue: And I want to say on behalf of our family, thank you for your service to our country and your contributions to your profession and your ongoing contributions to learning and this great effort of better thinking—critical thinking. So thank you, sweetheart.

Kevin: And thank you. I've enjoyed it immensely; it's been fun.

Sue: Me too.

Captain Kevin Smith and his wife, Sue, discussing his career in a video interview.

A US Navy Reserve Vought F-8J Crusader (BuNo 150317) of Fighter
Squadron VF-301 in flight between 1970 and 1973. US Navy National
Museum of Naval Aviation photo.

A US Navy McDonnell Douglas F-4N Phantom II (BuNo 152317) from
Fighter Squadron VF-111 "Sundowners" with Bicentennial markings in
flight. VF-111 was assigned to Carrier Air Wing 19 (CVW-19) aboard
the aircraft carrier USS *Franklin D. Roosevelt* (CV-42) for a deployment
to the Mediterranean Sea from 4 October 1976 to 21 April 1977. US
Navy National Museum of Naval Aviation photo.

THE PERCH

And [I have] done a hundred things you have never dreamed of.
—Pilot Officer John Magee Jr., Royal Canadian Air Force

WELL, I FOUND MYSELF "ON THE PERCH." THIS WAS ONE OF MANY positions that I was going to achieve. It was a starting position pretty high up. It was up there in the rarified part of the atmosphere at 35,000 feet. I was in this rather impressive machine—this was the sleek, fairly modern airplane that was capable of supersonic flight. The first one actually.

How did I get here? From a big-picture perspective, I got here primarily because of the experiences that we had gained during the latter stages of World War II. During that time, we developed and introduced the P-51 Mustang. Originally, the P-51 Mustang was a bit underpowered, but fortunately, there were some people that came forward with a better idea that the airplane could probably perform much better if it had a more powerful engine. The engine was already in existence; it didn't have to be developed. So that was good news.

The engine was a Rolls-Royce Merlin engine, and it was being used in the Supermarine Spitfire as well as the Lancaster bomber. Now what made this engine rather impressive was it was one of the first engines that was a V-12-piston engine, and one of the first engines that was outfitted with a two-stage supercharger—and that enabled it to perform well at high altitudes. It performed better at high altitudes than any other airplane of its day.

The P-51 airplane was designed with a modern airfoil or wing. The technical term for the airfoil was "laminar-flow." The laminar-flow wing combined with the Rolls-Royce Merlin engine produced an airplane with extraordinary performance. It could outperform any airplane in the sky at the time—to the tune of more than 100 knots. It could accelerate quickly and had quite a long range. Laminar-flow wings produced less drag so the range of the airplane was considerable.

It became the fighter airplane of the day. It performed so well that the Allied bomber forces were successful in bringing World War II in the European theater to a close because of their devastating effect, allowing the bombers to prevail.

So the takeaway from that is that if we had an airplane that could perform well at low, medium, and high altitudes; go fast; and could be maneuvered rather quickly—then we had something that could prevail in combat. After World War II, there was a massive national effort to achieve supersonic flight. And NASA, or what became NASA, along with the industry, got together and decided they were going to run some major flight experiments out of Edwards Air Force Base. Chuck Yeager was involved in that. As I record this, Chuck Yeager has recently passed away. We honor his memory. He was a remarkable individual and quite a national hero. He, along with his team of aerodynamic experts and scientists, was trying to get his airplane to go supersonically without falling apart, coming unglued, disintegrating, or going into a spin or other uncontrolled flight. And they were able to do that through various experimentations with a rocket-powered airplane. This was an experimental airplane, not a production-line airplane.

A lot was learned from this experimentation. A huge amount of information was gathered in terms of the ability to go supersonically. It made it at least feasible that we could actually, someday, engage in sonic warfare. Sonic warfare is our ability to conduct combat operations near, at, or beyond the speed of sound. That was particularly important back then. It was a huge national effort to build airplanes that were combat-capable that could operate near, at, or beyond the speed of sound.

There are a lot of things that happen from a physics standpoint and from an aerodynamic standpoint near, at, and beyond the speed of sound. A lot of strange things happened in this realm of flight. Things were discontinuous; the properties of the air changed dramatically, and the ability to control an object such as an aircraft became extremely difficult. The ability to control the airplane is a serious challenge not only for the designers but also for the pilots who are flying such a high-speed and agile machine. Agility had to be built into the aircraft. The aircraft had to be highly maneuverable for it to succeed in sonic warfare. That produced all kinds of challenges.

At the end of this era, we began to build sonic aircraft in enormous numbers; this was typically called the century-series era. The Air Force started to build such tactical airplanes, starting with the F-100, first introduced in 1954. The F-100, which is the Super Sabre, was a supersonic airplane—one of the first. They continued to build these century-series airplanes that had numbers associated with them that were in the hundreds. There was the F-100, F-102, F-104, F-106, and so on. There was also the B-58 Hustler, which was a supersonic bomber. All of these were quite extraordinary achievements.

The Navy had the F-11 Tiger, which was actually the world's first supersonic airplane. The F-11 Tiger was followed quickly by the F-8 Crusader, which was an extraordinarily fast and highly maneuverable airplane. The F-8 Crusader was at one time the world's fastest airplane, having exceeded 1,000 miles per hour. That was about Mach 1.6. It set lots of records. One of them still stands that was set by John Glenn. It was a coast-to-coast speed record in less than 3.5 hours. It also won the Collier and Thompson trophies. These were quite amazing achievements. It took a lot of training and various mental attributes for the pilots to fly such aircraft, which was not typically easy to do.

I was in advanced flight training as part of the United States Naval Air Academy. At that time, flight training had its own supersonic pipeline. I was in the F-11 Tiger, the first supersonic production airplane ever built. It was small, lightweight, and had a single cockpit (so it was flown by a single pilot). It could go through the sound barrier and achieve supersonic flight in the vicinity of about Mach 1.2. It was built and entered service with the Navy in about 1955. It was followed quickly by the F-8 Crusader, which was a significant improvement in lots of ways, so the F-11 Tiger saw a brief service operationally. It was retained as an advanced trainer, and that's how I got to fly it. Although it was a single-seat fighter, there were no trainer models of it, so your first flight in the F-11 was a solo flight.

The F-11 Tiger was used by the Blue Angels from 1957 to 1969. The Blue Angels certainly loved the airplane; the crowds loved it. It was a beautiful airplane. It did a rather impressive job with the Blue Angels.

The F-11 Tiger was built by Grumman Aerospace. It had a J65 engine—a Westinghouse engine. It was actually originally designed by the British, but it was being produced under license by Westinghouse. It was an early version of a turbojet and had an afterburner. The J65 engine was not originally designed to include afterburner capabilities. I think a lot of it was like, "We're rushing things, we were trying to get supersonic airplanes up and employed operationally," and so they put an afterburner on the J65 engine, and it improved the thrust. With the afterburner there was a little over 10,000 pounds of total thrust. It was a pretty good thrust-to-weight ratio. The airplane was outfitted for operational flight and weighed about 18,000 pounds.

The airplane had a thin wing—slight camber on top and flat on the bottom, so it could very easily go supersonically. It had some unusual control features associated with it, like no ailerons. The wing was 250 square feet in area and was swept back about 35 degrees— these are technical terms, but most aviators understand them. It had a rather interesting tail configuration, and it was fairly straightforward in flying. It flew pretty well. There were some issues in going through the sound barrier or going at the speed of sound. At the speed of sound, there are a lot of compressibility effects. The air becomes fairly turbulent. All kinds of strange things happen. Once you get through the speed of sound, things smooth out and become easier and a little bit more predictable. The flying qualities of the airplane in the transonic realm are fairly difficult. Most airplanes feel unstable, but we were able to figure out aerodynamically how to prevent that instability from occurring. Once it passes through that small band of the transonic, then it becomes more stable and predictable and consequently a bit easier to handle for the pilot.

Let's press on now with our story. I'm in the F-11 Tiger at the perch. This particular maneuver has lots of signified anchor points we can identify as we engage in precision maneuvering with the supersonic airplane. To execute this maneuver with precision, it has to be done to exacting standards. There's a small margin of error, so we've identified a number of anchor points in this particular maneuver.

The maneuver—air-to-air gunnery—begins at the perch (see Appendix A). This is a gunnery-training event, and this airplane is equipped with 20-millimeter cannons. I did this maneuver on a regular basis throughout my career because of the advanced supersonic pipeline that I was flying. This learning process was ongoing. It was continuously repeated during the course of a career of an early fighter pilot or early supersonic fighter pilot.

Our job in aerial combat was to prevail: defeat enemy forces that also have capable and sophisticated aircraft. Our job was to learn how to employ these weapons systems that we carry—these 20-millimeter cannons—so we had to figure out how to employ them effectively so as to neutralize, destroy, or shoot down enemy aircraft who were threatening us, our nation, or our combat forces. Our job was to gain control of the airspace above the battlefield. That was a particularly important job and responsibility we had as fighter pilots. The common term today that is being used—not entirely correctly, but that's the way things happen in any kind of a culture—is the Top Gun pilot.

So a Top Gun pilot and fighter pilot are more or less synonymous. We didn't use it then, but thanks to the *Top Gun* movie, everybody now understands in one way or another what that means. It means that these pilots are considered to be fighter pilots, and a fighter pilot's job is to shoot down other aircraft—enemy aircraft. It could be similar aircraft—that is, fighter against fighter, it could be fighter against bomber, it could be fighter against observation airplanes—whatever the enemy has put in the air is fair game for the fighter pilots.

The idea was to learn the art and skill of being a fighter pilot. None of what we did was perfect because a lot of things that we were doing had never been done before by humans, and so there was a lot of trial and error. We thought it was a pretty good idea to perform this advanced maneuver that we called "the gun pattern." The gun pattern consisted of about four fighter aircraft. They were all separated from one another, so they were not in close formation, but they were flying in the same pattern. The pattern occupied a fairly large space. They could actually be in the same airspace with one another if they knew where each airplane was. There were certain protocols in place to announce where we were so that the airplanes around us could keep their distance and maintain proper separation, avoiding a mid-air collision.

The gun pattern had what we call "the tractor." The tractor was actually an airplane pulling a gigantic banner. You've seen these advertising banners that are pulled by airplanes over beaches. It's basically the same thing. The big banner was about 1,500 feet behind the tractor, so there was a fairly large separation between the airplanes for protection. The banner was our designated target. Our job as fighter pilots in this maneuver was to get into a firing position on this simulated airborne enemy and to fire our guns into the banner in such a way that eventually we could record the number of hits we got on the banner. The number of bullets or cannons' projectiles that were positioned on the banner represented a hit to an enemy airplane. This maneuver was very complicated and took a lot of time and practice. We did this often in our training. Prior to getting our aviator wings, and even after getting aviator wings, we did the same thing.

The perch is the place where we are going to roll in on the target. Now the "roll in" is a fairly difficult maneuver because we are positioned abeam the tractor. We're going to roll in and roll away from our current position, and we're going to descend. We're going to do a rolling, descending maneuver. We're going to utilize an afterburner, and at some point in time we will actually go supersonically, so we will go through the sound barrier, and during our final engagement with this simulated enemy aircraft, we will be supersonic. We will be positioning ourselves and we will begin to fire our weapons systems—fire our guns—at the simulated enemy aircraft while we are traveling supersonically.

This is difficult because when you are at the speed of sound, the aircraft does not behave predictably! It goes through some kind of a transition where things become a bit unpredictable. It has to do with what's called "compressibility effect." The shock waves produce some kind of strange phenomena with respect to objects traveling at that speed. So it's a rather tricky part of the maneuver. We had to really work at trying to do the best we possibly could as Sonic Warriors to smooth out any turbulence and to predict as best we could what was going to be the best position to achieve success in this particular combat environment.

Success required precise maneuvering—very, very precise. It also required commitment, enormous focus, as well as very smooth, non-jerky applications of the controls. That required an enormous amount of practice and self-confidence. To be able to operate in this regime *smoothly* is a rather difficult thing to do. We had to get to the point where we were smooth as silk. We also had to be very committed to achieving the success that we had to have if we were going to prevail in combat.

Once we left the perch, we made our reversal. There are three points in the maneuver: the perch, the high reversal, and the low reversal. We made our high reversal, and then we're at the low reversal. The low reversal is the real test of aviation skills—this is where you go supersonic. The airplane goes from subsonic, transonic, to supersonic, and back. Because we're pulling Gs, we'll actually decelerate to a certain point, and so we're going back down through the supersonic, transonic, back to high subsonic. So we went through it, and now we're going back. That double transition made it very difficult to control the airplane precisely, and that's what was needed. We had to figure out—and we did eventually—ways in which we could make that transition from subsonic to supersonic back to subsonic in a short period of time and still maintain good tracking solutions on the simulated enemy target. It became a rather tricky thing. It is something that we worked on very, very hard. From my perspective, most of us became really quite good at doing this kind of maneuver.

In the broad context, we were doing what eventually became known as "maneuver warfare." We were at the ground floor of this rather impressive and significant movement in the annals of warfare. It was popularized by Colonel John Boyd, United States Air Force, who was also an expert in the gun pattern, or air-to-air gunnery. He taught that at Nellis Air Force Base for many years. He considered what we were doing to be nothing less than maneuver warfare, and he created this whole body of knowledge called maneuver-warfare theory, which exists today. It is a proven aspect of combat, being an important component of our combat thinking and our combat employment.

We were at the leading edge of this effort. Through various ways and our strong commitments, we were able to do maneuvers in a particularly good way. We became quite proficient in air-to-air gunnery. This difficult skill set was essential for national defense. We had to have this skill set; it was not optional. If, as a country, we were going to prevail and prevent enemies from defeating us like they tried to do during World War II, we had to have this skill set. They were extremely committed to defeating the United States in World War II. In a lot of cases, they came perilously close to defeating us in battle. They were not able to do so, but it wasn't because they didn't try hard enough. If we were going to keep that from becoming a reality after World War II, and after the Korean War, we had to become very skilled in air-to-air gunnery, or aerial combat.

We eventually were able to employ short-range missiles. They were developed shortly after this. So the fighter airplanes that I flew eventually had guns *and* missiles. The missiles were actually sidewinders; they were a major advancement in aerial combat. They were a very light, short-range missile. They didn't produce a lot of drag. We used the same kind of performance maneuvers with the missiles in aerial performance capabilities that we had with guns, and so we were able to refine this whole concept of maneuver warfare. We called it air-combat maneuvering, or ACM. It was our ability to maneuver in such a way as to defeat airborne enemy forces.

At the perch, I was getting ready to roll in, and I was aligning myself with the tractor. I then rolled the airplane to the left in about a 60-degree angle bank. Then I completed my high reversal. Immediately after I completed my high reversal, I was descending in afterburner and going very fast. And the high reversal was followed quickly by the low reversal, where I changed directions again. During a low reversal, you achieve your tracking solution on the simulated airborne enemy platform. A low reversal is where you go supersonically, so supersonic flight was a factor in achieving our tracking solutions.

We had to be able to anticipate what the airplane was going to do. The airplane had some pitching moments that had to be anticipated and dealt with effectively. At some point during the low reversal, we would fire our guns at the banner. The duration of firing was only a few seconds because of the speed you're at. So after we completed our firing, we broke off from the maneuver and positioned ourselves to fly parallel to the tractor. Once we were parallel to, but offset left from the tractor, then we pitched up and went back up to the perch. We did that repeatedly in this exercise. We did this maneuver repeatedly, but eventually, we would get to a low-fuel state, and we would have to return to base. We could do about four of these maneuvers in one flight session.

The air-to-air gunnery maneuver was something that was a major part of the life of a Top Gun pilot and Sonic Warrior. We had to be able to do that maneuver, and we had to be able to do it well. The aerial gunnery maneuver that we performed, practiced, and got good at taught us all kinds of things. We gained self-confidence knowing that we could actually do such a complicated maneuver and become successful. The other thing is that most of us soon became really quite comfortable in the airplane. The airplane and the pilot became as one.

We were working together. We knew what the airplane could do, and we were friendly and comfortable with the airplane. It became our home away from home. It was stressful but also an enjoyable place to be. I felt that: "This is where I belong." This airplane I was flying was quite capable, responsive, and fairly forgiving in terms of how it would not do things that were drastically outside the box. You could understand it and it could understand you. I'm not sure there was much transfer from machine to the man, but the human and machine became as one. We also called it "seat of the pants" flying. There was something in the ability to understand the aircraft intuitively, and that became a particularly important aspect of our work—that's what we learned first and foremost. That's where I learned key flying aspects of becoming a Sonic Warrior. This is where I began my career. This is where I was becoming a proficient Sonic Warrior.

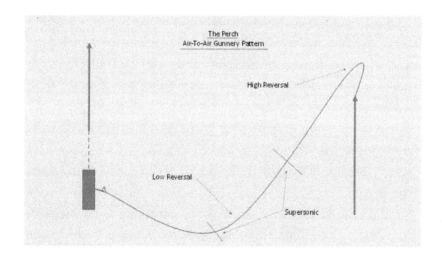

A Grumman F11F-1 Tiger fighter on display at the US Museum of Naval Aviation at Pensacola (Florida). Aircraft BuNo 141828 is painted in the colors of Fighter Squadron VF-33 *Astronauts* in 1959, when the squadron was deployed as part of *Carrier Air Group Six (CVG-6)* (tail code "AF") aboard the aircraft carrier USS *Intrepid (CVA-11)* to the Mediterranean Sea. US Museum of Naval Aviation photo.

EPISODE 3

SPEED RUN

"FOR A SPEED RUN." THAT'S ABOUT ALL IT SAID. I WAS SCHEDULED to fly an F-8 Crusader. This was back when they were new. They were the frontline fighters of the US Navy, they were carrier-based, and they were seriously supersonic. They were really fast. "Supersonic" didn't tell the whole story because they were *amazingly* supersonic. And at one time they were the fastest airplane in the world.

I was at the Naval Air Station Cecil Field, in northern Florida, near Jacksonville. I was in VF-174 squadron. That was the F-8 weapons system readiness training squadron. There are a number of terms that we used for that. In the Navy we used the term F-8 RAG. RAG is an acronym for Replacement Air Group. The RAG was used for transitioning to a particular weapons system, and it was a transition program to get pilots combat qualified. These pilots were recent graduates of the Naval Air Academy. I was going through this combat-qualification program with this advanced-training squadron. We were using frontline fighters—the F-8 Crusader—and we were scheduled for a speed run.

Why were we doing this? For two reasons: number one was to be awarded the 1,000-mph pin. Number two: to learn how this airplane handled at high supersonic speeds. The high supersonic speed is approximately Mach 1.5. It was higher than that, but generally speaking, it was in the Mach 1.5 regime, which is 1.5 times the speed of sound. For an airplane to go faster than the speed of sound, it took quite a bit of aerodynamic sophistication and aerodynamic

55

improvements. There were a whole lot of things that were being learned during that period of time because this was really the beginning of the supersonic era. Supersonic flight was being pursued by a number of organizations including the Air Force, the Naval Air Force, and the Marine Corps. The supersonic flying environment was becoming more and more popular, notwithstanding the fact that it was challenging and often dangerous.

The airplane that I was about ready to climb into was the F-8 Crusader. It was the F-8 Echo, which was the latest version of the airplane, so it was basically brand-new at the time—right off the production line. And the Echo was an improvement of the original airplane. They went through a number of improvements, going from A all the way up to E. Each letter designated a particular improved version of the last one. This airplane had a more powerful engine. It had some improvements in the radar and weapons systems, and it carried missiles and guns.

This is a single-seat airplane. There is no trainer version of it, so I was going out there on a speed run *solo*. But I was being chased by a senior instructor pilot. The chase pilot is the seasoned instructor pilot who is there for safety reasons. He was going to be flying my wing, and I was going to be going "out there" to the military operating area off the coast of northern Florida. It was a designated area where only military airplanes could operate. You had to have special clearances to do that.

We were going to do the speed run over the ocean because we were going to create an enormous sonic boom, which would have been felt on the ground and would have broken windows if we did that over land. We were over the ocean to avoid that kind of situation. The civilian population wasn't particularly fond of having sonic booms. This disturbed their day-to-day activities.

We were getting ready; we strapped on the airplanes, we took off, we proceeded to go to this military operating area, and we set up for the speed run. To set it up, we climbed to 35,000 feet. Essentially, we were going to duplicate the official speed run that was conducted at Edwards Air Force Base. It was official, it was sanctioned, and it was instrumented. The official speed run for the F-8 Crusader was conducted in the late 1950s; my speed run that I was involved with occurred in 1965. But in the late 1950s, a Crusader was hot off the production line. It was a brand-new airplane, and it was seriously fast. It was eye-watering in the speed that it could achieve. During its official speed run, it broke a number of speed records and was at that time the fastest airplane in the world. It was the only airplane flying at that time that was able to exceed 1,000 miles per hour.

The F-8 Crusader set a number of speed records. It also won the Collier and the Thompson trophies. It was also fast in terms of its ability to accelerate. The F-8 Crusader's ability to accelerate was nothing short of phenomenal. This phenomenal ability enabled the airplane—at the altitudes that I was going to conduct a speed run—to accelerate at 50 knots per second up to about 600+ knots. That was beyond the speed of sound in the order of Mach 1.2 to 1.4.

Another record that it set, which still stands today, was a coast-to-coast speed run set by John Glenn in an F-8 Crusader, which was called Project Bullet, conducted in 1957. It was quite an achievement. The average speed of that flight was about Mach 1.2. They did have to refuel a couple of times, but when you average the speed out, they averaged about Mach 1.2 over the continental United States. The refueling was done in the air—in-flight refueling—so the airplane never did land, but it did have to slow down for a short period of time.

Why did we want to go fast? What was this need for speed? The need for speed was predicated on the ability of the airplane to outperform all other airplanes, especially the airplanes by our arch enemy. Those enemy airplanes were sophisticated and fast. We wanted our airplanes to be faster and primarily more lethal, which means that we wanted the airplanes to be fast and highly maneuverable. We also wanted the airplanes that we flew to be carrier-based in some cases. The enemy never did have any carrier-based aircraft or a carrier-based fighter force. So the need for speed was essential. You can argue that was essential for our survival as a nation.

I was going to duplicate the official speed run of the 1950s. I was going to get up to 1,000 miles per hour. In doing so, I was going to be awarded the 1,000 MPH pin, which I would then be able to pin on my uniform or lapel if I were wearing civilian clothes. We're going to take a full load of gas, we're going to go into afterburner, we're going to stay in afterburner for a long time, and we're going to see how fast we can actually get the airplane to go in this special military operating area. So I proceeded to do that. We climbed up to 35,000 feet, and we got set up for the speed run: we checked our instruments, we checked our position and navigation displays, and we checked the area. We had long-range airborne radar working with us to make sure that we didn't have any stray airplanes going through this military operating area, so the chance of in-flight collisions was pretty much minimal.

How was this airplane able to do such a thing, and what were the innovations that enabled this airplane in an early part of its career to be the fastest airplane in the world? What were the innovations?

The first thing is the ability of the airplane to go fast—it is predicated largely, but not exclusively, on the wing design. There was a major breakthrough in aerodynamic technology that made this possible. The wing design of the F-8 Crusader was like nothing else that had ever been done before. The wing was highly swept. It was approximately at a 45-degree angle. And it was fairly thin, which means that the transonic drag was reduced. During the period where the airplane is going from subsonic to supersonic flight, there is considerable transonic drag rise. This airplane was designed to minimize the transonic drag rise. Once the airplane gets into the supersonic area, the drag reduces or decreases somewhat until you go extremely fast—until you get above Mach 2.0. This transonic drag rise had to be dealt with, and the F-8 Crusader was able to deal with this transonic drag rise better than most other airplanes.

Even today we could say that the F-8 Crusader's ability to move through the transonic regime with minimum drag rise has never been duplicated and has never been beaten. That's because there were a number of innovations that were in place, not least of which were some

58

of the things that were developed by NASA during that period of time. They did a lot of work in the area of supersonic flight. A lot of ideas, breakthroughs, and equations were developed by NASA, working closely with the military. This was the great time where government-industry collaboration produced very fruitful results.

So the wing was particularly important. It was a marvelous piece of aerodynamic engineering. It was highly swept, and it had a saw-tooth leading-edge feature to it, which enabled it to achieve things that could not ordinarily be achieved. It was a flexible wing, and the wing area was pretty much optimum. The wing area was about 325 square feet. And that, by many, including John Boyd, was considered to be quite an optimum size for a fighter aircraft.

The control system was set up to maximize flight, not only subsonic but also to maximize controllability in the supersonic regime. The fuselage was long, which was helpful because it also enabled it to achieve a favorable fineness ratio. Fineness ratio is a technical term that basically means the width versus the length. If you had a fairly long but fairly thin body, it would go fast in the atmosphere as well as in the ocean. The fineness ratio helps a lot of fish swim fast.

The F-8 had a long fuselage, and it carried all of this fuel internally. And this is probably the most important thing: *the F-8 Crusader carried all of its fuel internally.* There was no external fuel tank ever used in the airplane. So for its long service life, which exceeded thirty years in all cases, it carried all of its fuel internally. That enabled it to be extremely fast and maneuverable under all conditions that it was used. It carried a fair amount of fuel internally—somewhere in the area of about 10,000 pounds of fuel. It was quite good in that respect.

The control systems were set up that enabled us to operate during these regimes where control sensitivity was in fact an issue. It had some roll and yaw stabilization. It really was a joy to fly. It was a bit high strung and a bit sensitive. In some cases, you had to be light on the controls. Nevertheless, it performed extremely well, and the engine was in fact a marvel. The engine was a Pratt & Whitney J57. There were various versions of that. The version I was flying was a J57-P20.

The P20 was at that time the latest version, a little bit more powerful than the early version. It was really quite a marvelous engine. It was very reliable and powerful, and it could handle all kinds of situations and not degrade itself. It was very hard to get the engine to stall. You could also go into afterburner until you ran out of fuel. You didn't normally do that of course. All of us Crusader pilots were very happy with this engine because of its capabilities in the flight envelope and extraordinary reliability, which was necessary for any single-engine aircraft. It was quite a marvelous piece of work and a great credit to this wonderful company called Pratt & Whitney Aircraft Engines. They spent a lot of time and effort building reliable engines.

The ability to accelerate was probably its greatest feature. The acceleration rate was not normally part of an officially sanctioned speed run, and that's unfortunate. I think we should also be looking at not just the terminal speed of the airplane but at how quickly it could achieve that speed. The acceleration rate and the acceleration over the full operating environment or envelope are particularly important as well. And this airplane was probably the fastest accelerating airplane. It certainly was in the Navy, and it may very well have been across the board for all airplanes.

I would also give the F-104 credit for being extremely fast, and it may very well have been capable of a greater acceleration than the F-8 Crusader. It had very limited capabilities, and so the Air Force didn't use it for very long. But the F-8 Crusader stood the test of time because it was so effective at what it did.

On this speed run, I had selected afterburner, and there were a couple of things I had to do. I got to go supersonic very quickly. The transition from transonic to supersonic in this airplane was very mild. There wasn't a lot of buffering, and there weren't a lot of control abnormalities that occurred. There were some slight changes in the control capabilities in the airplane, but it went pretty much through the sound barrier mostly undisturbed. Once I got above Mach 1.2, an interesting thing happened—everything became eerily quiet. That is because the speed of sound is now behind you. You are traveling *faster* than the speed of sound, and everything that is making noise is behind you because you're out in front of the sound so far that you actually don't hear anything. And so everything becomes quite quiet.

We were accelerating down to somewhere in the vicinity of probably 25,000 feet, and we climbed back up again to 35,000 feet, and then we pushed it over again to descend a little bit so we could accelerate quicker. And we were able to get to 1,000 miles per hour, which is about Mach 1.6. We got up to Mach 1.6, and then that was pretty much it. We came out of afterburner, we descended, and we then proceeded back to our home base. When we got down from the flight, we calculated that, indeed, we had exceeded 1,000 miles per hour (we had to convert a couple of things), and then they awarded me the 1,000 MPH pin. For me, this was a special moment. I began to realize that I was a fighter pilot and a Sonic Warrior—it wasn't just a dream.

Now how does this help tactically? In a tactical environment, you're probably not going to go that fast, but the fact that you can actually go that fast is very useful. You can escape in an environment where you are so outnumbered that there isn't any point in engaging the enemy. That's probably the most important thing. And there's another reason why we would like our fighter aircraft to be extraordinarily fast—to accelerate at a blinding speed—for close-in-air combat. The F-8 Crusader did this better than most. Some may object to that assertion. But by and large the F-8 Crusader was the best in what it did for close-in-air combat. Most of us who flew the airplane and know about fighter airplanes would agree that in terms of close-in-air combat, the F-8 Crusader did that better than any other airplane. In particular, it did it better than our arch-enemies' airplane.

The F-8's control system was optimized for this kind of speed envelope rather nicely and very innovatively. The airplane was not entirely stable in all regimes. The airplane did exhibit neutral directional stability, but at high speeds of 700 knots and above, we did experience some instability, so we were instructed not to exceed 700 knots. That was well above what we would normally use anyway.

Speed was of course extremely important for all of us. To tactically pursue our enemies, to engage our enemies, and to succeed in combat, we were highly dependent on the ability of our aircraft to achieve very high speeds that were superior to the speeds of enemy aircraft. This airplane did it extremely well, and it did it for a very long period of time.

Picture of the coveted 1000 MPH Pin from LTV
Aerospace, received by Captain Smith in 1965.

MISSION CRITICAL

IN THE SUMMER OF **1968, I** WAS AT THE END OF A **12,000**-FOOT runway. This runway was part of the Naval Air Station Oceana in Virginia Beach, Virginia. I was waiting for two F-4 Phantoms, which were brand-new Navy fighters, to take off in front of me. I was planning to join up with them soon after takeoff. I was not in an F-4 Phantom II; I was in an F-8 Crusader. The F-8 Crusader was roughly a contemporary of the F-4 Phantom II. It was a few years ahead of the Phantom's fleet introduction and also a lightweight fighter. It carried guns and early missiles. These missiles were typically the sidewinder version of the missiles, which was a very successful design. It was designed by the Naval Weapons Center, China Lake, California.

After the F-4s took off and broke ground, I was given my takeoff clearance. So I lit my afterburner, rocketed down the runway, took off, and joined up with the flight of the two F-4 Phantoms. We proceeded out to a military operating area. It was off the coast of Virginia in the

Atlantic, so it was a fairly large military operating area. In this particular case, we were going to perform air-combat maneuvering—more specifically, close-in-air-combat maneuvering, which happened to be part of an advanced air combat training curriculum.

It is a fascinating story of why we were doing this. It is probably one of the most important stories in the history of military aviation. I would go so far as to say it is probably one of the most important stories in all of aviation. It turns out this was a very serious attempt to deal with a rather troubling and extremely serious problem, which we classified as mission critical. Mission critical is a term that means that something is very difficult and complex, but it is essential that it be done, such that it becomes critical to the mission. We were engaged in the mission-critical activity to upgrade the close-in-air combat skills of the F-4 Phantom flight crews. At that time, the Phantom was a brand-new airplane. It was entering the fleet to become the primary air-combat fighter for both the Navy and Air Force. The Air Force was in the process of purchasing a land-based version. The Navy had a carrier-based version, which required different structural modifications for it to perform well in a carrier environment.

This story is based upon the prevailing wisdom of the day, which happened to be fundamentally flawed. The prevailing wisdom said that in advancing technology in the field of missiles and missile-oriented technology, air-to-air missiles were going to quickly replace the cannons or guns we carried in the Crusader. Advancements were made on a regular basis, and these sophisticated air-to-air missiles, which in some cases were guided, were considered to be more effective in the air-combat environment. They were far more lethal and were maneuverable after they left the mother aircraft. It was thought that these missiles were going to replace the guns and therefore negate the need for close-in-air combat.

The missiles were going to extend the lethality range further out beyond the friendly aircraft or the friendly flight of other craft, probably beyond a hundred miles. It kind of depends on the era, missile, and particular airplane. The airborne radar system in the F-4 Phantom was new, and it was fairly long range. The lethality range for the Phantom was advertised as about fifty miles, maybe further. Some of it was of course classified at the time. Because it was thought that these modern missiles were going to negate the need for any kind of close-in-air combat involvement, close-in-air combat training was no longer being conducted by the F-4 Phantom II flight crews. Close-in-air combat maneuvering was quickly going to be superseded by longer-range missile-oriented combat.

Now up to this point, close-in-air combat maneuvering was a very important skill for all fighter pilots. It was taught and practiced continuously. It involved all kinds of various aspects, features, setups, and operational engagements across the spectrum. It was an extremely important skill. It was also very difficult in terms of the ability to perform in that environment because we were dealing with a four-dimensional problem space. Four-dimensional space is basically the XYZ-axis plus time. There is an x-, a y-, and a z-axis that forms a cube, so you're working within a cubicle space. The fourth dimension is time, which is very important. This cube moves and changes shape, but it actually moves along the time horizon. You cannot freeze the time. Four-dimensional space is a rather unusual place for a human to be. From a cognitive system standpoint, a human is not optimized to perform well in a four-dimensional space but can get good at it over time with training and practice.

Time is very important because the time that you are airborne also relates to the fuel that you have available in the aircraft. So the time-fuel factor is extremely important. All of these things have to be manipulated, coordinated, and combined together into some kind of a big picture. And it's a rather difficult thing. It can be taught, however. Humans can become pretty good at it with enough practice. There are examples of aces throughout aviation history, and these folks have been able, more or less, to perfect the art and science of close-in-air combat maneuvering.

Close-in-air combat maneuvering was invented during the latter stages of World War I. In World War II, it became an art form, particularly the latter stages of World War II when the P-51 was available to the fighter forces of the United States. Because of the P-51 and its magnificent performance characteristics, many of our American pilots performed extraordinarily well in that arena. It was really a breakthrough airplane. It enabled close-in-air combat to move into the high-speed realm. It became the precursor of the Sonic Warrior era. It was not supersonic, but it got to be relatively fast. We're looking at 450 knots in air speed. That was quite a remarkable airplane for its day. Air-combat maneuvering was a major part of the fighter community up until the Phantom entered service with its weapons system and its relatively long-range missile system. The Phantom did not have guns; it was just equipped with missiles. The thinking was that the guns were unnecessary, and so they need not be installed in this modern fighter.

Remember, points of view are extremely important here. We're talking about a frame of reference, or what I like to say is "what occupies your mind space." What is it that occupies one's mind space? How did you come to that position in your understanding of things—your belief, your perception of reality—and how are you dealing with it going forward in time and space? The mind space, the perception, and the model of reality were that close-in-air-combat maneuvering was no longer necessary because we could defeat the enemy at a much longer range.

Then something happened along the way—the Vietnam conflict. Some people call it the Vietnam War. It was a regional conflict. I like to refer to it as the Vietnam conflict in the midst of the Cold War. I don't like to mix those terms together, because they were clearly related but somewhat different in many respects. The whole point of the Cold War was to prepare ourselves to defeat the enemy prior to hostilities. We were Cold War warriors trained in the key aspects of Cold War mentality.

One of the first major air campaigns since the Korean conflict was called Operation Rolling Thunder. Rolling Thunder was designed to bring the North Vietnamese leadership to the peace table to end this war early on. It turned out to be an eye opener for US forces from a number of perspectives. From the air-warfare perspective, Rolling Thunder showed that there were some serious weaknesses in our air-combat weapons systems. There was a crash program set up to try to understand why our performance was not up to our expectations. Why did the air-warfare component of our combat engagements not perform as expected and not perform very well at all? There were a whole bunch of things going on, so the key thing for all of us to understand was to clarify what was the actual problem, or what I call "clarify the actual." The first order of business is to not rush to conclusions or to a particular favorite solution but to spend a little bit of quality time up front studying the facts.

The problem was our air-combat weapons systems were simply not performing well. We were experiencing all kinds of difficulties and system failures, and our flight crews were not prepared for the environment. One observer (Ault) stated that we were using a heads-down system in our airplanes to fight a heads-up war. That pretty much summarizes the difficulties we were facing. The brand-new ten-million-dollar missile-equipped Phantom airplanes were not performing very well. The flight crews were not experienced in this kind of air combat. They were trained for long-range, and they were facing close-in, highly maneuverable, difficult-to-see targets. They were not employing effective maneuvering tactics and procedures to deal with such an engagement. The Navy decided that through some grassroots efforts it needed to understand fundamentally why our systems were not performing very well.

Captain Frank Ault, US Navy, was the former commanding officer of the USS *Coral Sea*. He was tasked with the responsibility of determining exactly why our air-combat resources were performing so poorly. The report that came from him as chairman of this investigative committee was the famous *Ault Report*. The official title of it was "Air-to-Air Missile System Capability Review." The findings of the *Ault Report* were quite chilling. It was a profoundly important document. I commend the work of Captain Ault and his team for doing a magnificent job of understanding and bringing to our attention a complete understanding of the problem.

The *Ault Report* uncovered a whole bunch of issues that needed to be dealt with. First and foremost was training readiness. The way we were training flight crews to achieve combat readiness was fundamentally flawed. We were not focusing on those areas we needed to improve or the skills and the mental attributes necessary to succeed in close-in-air combat. The ingredients for mission success were not understood all that well.

The most important thing we learned was that we did not understand the operational limitations of airborne missiles. We did not know what the missile-firing envelope was. We assumed the firing envelope was characterized as time-space A, but in actuality the envelope was characterized as time-space B, which was significantly different than what we thought it would be and should be. It seriously constrained our ability to defeat the enemy aircraft systems while airborne.

We had systems that we thought were highly lethal. As it turns out, they were not completely lethal except in the most ideal circumstances. The *Ault Report* also showed that our airborne radar systems and missile systems were not reliable at all. This report had some serious recommendations for reliability and lethality.

One example of the problem is that 80 percent of the missiles that were fired in combat engagements during Rolling Thunder were fired outside of the firing envelope, such that the missile then went ballistic and was not effective, could not guide, or was not in a position to destroy the airborne enemy platforms. Eighty percent of the missiles were fired outside of the missile-firing envelope! That was a serious flaw in our systems' performance. The reliability just was not there. These were very high-tech systems, but they were not robust in any way at all. This lack of robustness was a serious problem. Only one in ten missiles fired and left the airplane—one in ten! If you combine one in ten along with 80 percent, you can see that our war-fighting capabilities were severely hampered by such a deficient system.

Combine that with the fact that the flight crews were not trained or experienced in close-in-air combat because it was assumed that they would not have to engage in close-in-air combat. That proved to be a serious flaw in the thinking and proved to be a huge problem. That was most mission critical in this particular time and place for military aviation. It was so mission critical that a whole bunch of things were then put in motion. The first thing was the revamping of air-combat training for all fighter crews. It was the beginning of the Top Gun initiative. The Top Gun initiative included, but was not limited to, the Navy Fighter Weapons School set up at Naval Air Station Miramar, California. There were other things that related to the Top Gun movement—the *Have Doughnut* project, the *Ault Report*, and the *Red Baron* studies. The Naval Air Force, US Atlantic fleet, initiated a grassroots effort on the East Coast. They decided they needed to upgrade the close-in-air combat skills of the Phantom crews as quickly as possible because they were getting ready to deploy to Vietnam as soon as six months to a year.

A top-secret report called *Have Doughnut* came out around the same time as the *Ault Report*. It was produced by the test and evaluation squadron VX-4 based at NAS Point Mugu. *Have Doughnut* involved the operational evaluation of the Soviet-built MiG-21. The MiG-21 was the major adversary during the Vietnam conflict in terms of airborne fighter capabilities. It came out about the same time that the fighter community stationed at Naval Air Station Oceana, Virginia Beach, Virginia, was preparing to upgrade the fighter skills of the community there. They were very serious about upgrading close-in-air combat skills of the F-4 Phantom crews.

The *Have Doughnut* studies were conducted by VX-4 and, in particular, the pilot who flew the MiG-21 against all of the US-related airplanes was a friend of mine, Captain Bill Kiper. His studies revealed that from a performance standpoint the F-8 Crusader was closely related to the MiG-21. They were about the same at top-end speed. I believe that the MiG-21 was a bit faster than the F-8 Crusader at top end. Performance-wise, in a high-G environment, the F-8 Crusader performed somewhat better than the MiG-21. It was a pretty good trainer in terms of being able to train flight crews to fight and succeed against a relatively modern and highly maneuverable lightweight fighter like the MiG-21. Indeed, the F-8 Crusader was a great adversary trainer for the F-4 community.

The Naval Air Force US Atlantic Fleet Commander asked my F-8 squadron to help them out. Because I had quite a lot of hours in the F-8 Crusader, was experienced in key aspects of this aircraft, and was relatively experienced in the field of close-in-air combat, they chose me.

That's why I was going out to the military operating area with the flight of two F-4 Phantoms. These were pilots who were preparing for deployment in the next six months, but they had some time to train in the advanced air-combat arena. This training was pretty much a crash course. I was involved in training these flight crews to upgrade their close-in-air combat skills so that they could successfully engage and defeat the enemy aircraft that were being deployed in certain areas of North Vietnam. Many of the flight crews were going to encounter these particular airplanes that had these particular flying characteristics so similar to the F-8 Crusader.

We were going to perform what is called a 2v1. In fighter pilot lingo, this means that two F-4 Phantoms will engage a single adversary aircraft—in this case my F-8 Crusader. The two Phantoms were going to engage me in this environment in a very realistic close-in-air-combat engagement. We performed two engagements during this particular flight. The engagements involved very high-G maneuvering and lots of altitude gains and losses. It was high-G maneuvering for about half an hour to forty-five minutes. The flight duration was probably not much longer than an hour because we would quickly run out of gas when we were using the afterburner so frequently.

One of the key maneuvers that we were working on with Phantom crews was called a high-vertical maneuver. The high-vertical maneuver is often referred to as a loop version, or we would call it an oblique loop, but it was pitching up high in the vertical. The airplanes performed differently in the high-vertical environment. We had to be able to deal with those different aerodynamic characteristics. These were the particular maneuvers and activities, so vital for their mission success that we were engaged in, so that we could get the Phantom crews to perform well in an environment they didn't have a lot of experience in.

There were a lot of things we learned in the close-in-air combat maneuvering environment. This was a fairly new environment because we were using aircraft that were very high speed. All three aircraft—the F-4 Phantom II, the F-8 Crusader, and the MiG-21—were supersonic airplanes. They were airplanes that could easily exceed the speed of sound on a regular basis. We were now engaged in what I call sonic warfare—we were becoming Sonic Warriors. The reason is we were operating at or near the speed of sound, and sometimes we were beyond it! To give you an example, the F-8 Crusader that I was flying could actually exceed the speed of sound in level flight at 15,000 feet in basic engine. Basic engine means non-afterburner operation. That's an extraordinary achievement in any era. *This airplane was so incredibly fast.*

The F-8 Crusader could easily go through the speed of sound with not even a fare-thee-well. It was also highly maneuverable because it had a very advanced wing design. The F-8 Crusader had a better wing design than the Phantom or the MiG-21. The MiG-21 had a rather primitive wing design. The Phantom had a better wing design, but the F-8 Crusader had the best wing design. You could argue that the F-8 Crusader remains one of the best wing designs ever in the history of aviation.

We worked hard every day in this mission-critical activity for at least a year, helping these flight crews improve their air-combat maneuvering capabilities within the aspects of close-in-air combat. We were quite successful. Others attempted to improve the reliability of the weapons systems and teach flight crews the missile-firing envelope. Those things were going along simultaneously with the efforts that I was engaged in. We produced flight crews that were extremely cred-ible in the close-in-air combat arena, and they proved themselves to be credible during the subsequent major air activities during the 1972 era.

AERIAL COMBAT

Up, up the long, delirious burning blue
I've topped the wind-swept heights with easy grace,
where never lark, or even eagle, flew.

—Flight Lieutenant John Magee Jr., Royal Canadian Air Force

Naval Air Station Oceana, Virginia Beach, Virginia, 1968

I WAS AT THE SQUADRON IN THE FLIGHT PLANNING ROOM, AND IT was late afternoon. Spread out on the table before me were three key documents: the first one was the early draft of the *Ault Report*, the second one was the tactics manual of the fighter aircraft that I was flying, and the third one was a secret report titled *Have Doughnut* that was produced by VX-4 out of Naval Air Station Point Mugu, California.

I had also become familiar with verbal reports from pilots returning from the first air campaign of the Vietnam conflict called Rolling Thunder. Now the tactics manual and the *Have Doughnut* report were secret documents, so I had to remain at the squadron with them. I could not take them out of the squadron spaces. This was late afternoon, and it looked like it was going to be a long night, but the Officers Club would be serving food until 10:00 p.m., so I figured I would have a late dinner after I finished my investigation and preparation. Tomorrow was a big day. It was one of these special events or occasions that you occasionally encounter in your work life. This day marked the beginning of the Top Gun initiative for the Naval Air Force, US Atlantic fleet. The mission statement for this initiative was to upgrade the close-in-air-combat capabilities of the F-4 Phantom II flight crews since this area had been seriously neglected in their training up to this point.

The Atlantic fleet version of the Top Gun initiative employed the F-8 Crusader as the adversary aircraft to perform this close-in-air combat training. Its performance characteristics closely matched the MiG-21, the enemy aircraft most concerning to US forces at that time.

I call some key members of the Top Gun initiative Top Gun pioneers. There are a number of important people that we should all be aware of and show our gratitude for the magnificent work that they did to upgrade our air-combat capabilities of US Air Forces: the Air Force, the Navy, and the Marines. One of the Top Gun pioneers we should all recognize is Captain Bill Kiper, US Navy. He was the first American pilot to fly the MiG-21, and he was able to examine this performance with respect to many other airplanes in our arsenal at that time. This was quite an accomplishment. He and the leadership of VX-4 authored this important *Have Doughnut* document that I was reading, and it set the stage for everything to follow.

Air-to-air combat is a particular form of combat that was first employed in World War I. Air-to-air combat is basically a friendly or adversary, single or group of airplanes that are trying to defeat one another. It means basically neutralizing—shooting down if you will—the enemy military assets that are airborne. It can be called aerial combat or air-combat maneuvering. I want to make a distinction between aerial combat and air combat. Aerial combat is air-to-air combat engagements which means airplanes are fighting each other. Air combat can be conducting warfare from the air and includes such things as air-to-ground bombing, strafing, reconnaissance, and electronic warfare.

ACM is a little bit of a misnomer because before you begin to execute a particular maneuver in the air-combat arena, there needs to be a fair amount of preparation before the maneuver is executed.

Often many of our documents and much of our training either treated planning and preparing inadequately or completely ignored them. The preparation and planning stage is extremely important.

How do you prepare? How do you prepare yourself? How do you prepare your subordinates, or in this case your wingmen? How do you prepare them for this rather difficult form of combat?

This form of combat is not only difficult, but it's actually fairly unusual for humans. Humans are not normally experienced in or trained to perform exacting activities in four dimensions. Humans are pretty good in two-dimensional space, we're not particularly good working in three-dimensional space, and we are mostly unprepared to deal with four-dimensional space. Four dimensions, in fighter-pilot terms, are the x-, y-, and z-axes plus time. The x-, y-, and z-axes make a cubic three-dimensional battlespace. The fourth dimension is the fact that everything is moving—the battlespace will move geographically, and everything within this cubicle construct will move, change, warp, and displace with respect to time. Time is directly related to fuel because you are burning fuel, and fuel will last only for a certain period of time. The fuel (or the chemical energy that you have at your disposal) is the internal fuel or the fuel aboard the aircraft.

It's critical to be able to understand, think, and solve problems in four-dimensional space. To give you an idea of the complexity of this particular environment, we can examine the "three-body problem." This is in theoretical physics or theoretical mathematics. (See Appendix B for more information on the three-body problem.)

The three-body problem is something that is difficult to imagine, and it's even more difficult to deal with in a very specific and exacting way. The three-body problem is a situation in which there is no deterministic solution. It represents areas of uncertainty where we don't have mathematics, theories, or that which is necessary to come up with a distinct solution every time. It's more of a probability in terms of what is the likelihood of something to occur in the future given a particular set of circumstances in the present. In this case, we're talking about a *four-body problem* because we're in four dimensions.

We're dealing with an arena here that is fraught with uncertainty. There is a high level of uncertainty and other factors entering into this. The individual who brought this all out into the operational community was a remarkable individual by the name of Colonel John Boyd, US Air Force. He brought this whole area of theoretical concepts, theoretical physics, and theoretical mathematics into the operational community. He explained how we could understand the operational complexities better if we had a working knowledge of things like uncertainty, incompleteness, probabilities, and other aspects of non-determinism. We cannot solve an air-combat problem deterministically because there are way too many variables. The best we can do is to come up with something that has a higher probability of success than whatever is conceptualized by our enemies.

We need the ability to engage in *higher order reasoning* that is significantly better, or significantly more capable, than our enemies. So our higher order reasoning becomes the order of the day. What exactly is that? It's one of the keys to success in this particular arena. We have to employ higher order reasoning. We have to be proficient in it to a certain extent, and we have to basically employ it in order for us to truly understand what's going on, to clarify the actual, to be able to predict future situations from current events, to solve the battle problem, and to succeed in conflict.

There are four key areas with respect to aerial combat. First is preparation—to always be prepared. That's the Boy Scout motto. We have to be prepared well before we actually engage the enemy. The second thing is we have to achieve the advantage. This is extremely important. Before we execute a particular maneuver, we have to achieve an advantageous position. We have to have sufficient energy in terms of velocity; we have to have an advantageous position with respect to altitude. Altitude relates to potential energy, and our fuel aboard has to be equal to or better in terms of duration than our enemy.

Third, after we achieve the advantage, we can engage the enemy in a certain way. There are some prescribed maneuvers, engagement tactics, and engagement strategies. They are somewhat different from each other, but the engagement follows a general construct of a set of maneuvers. These maneuvers can be modified or altered accordingly. That's fairly complicated, and it does require a fair amount of training and experience to be able to do that.

So we engage the enemy by executing a particular maneuver, a series of maneuvers, or a modification of a single maneuver or a set of maneuvers. The maneuver has to deal with displacement, altitude, speed, advantage, and the agility of the man-machine system. Agility is important when considering the amount of G-forces that are available to you and your aircraft.

Finally, the last thing needed to succeed in conflict is to deploy the weapons system in an area where there is a very high probability that it will destroy or damage the enemy aircraft.

There are two "performance tables" that we need to consider. The first performance table represents the factors that influence air-combat performance from the machine standpoint. The second performance table represents factors that contribute to or influence air-combat performance from the human perspective. So here we have the human and the machine that are working together. We have a human-machine interface and a human-machine system that are performing certain complex operations. It is very important to look at it from this perspective. How should one consider this system going forward? Is it suitable? Is it optimized for the environment? Is it set up successfully to solve complex operations?

Mission Performance Table
Information Management
Energy Management
Crew Resource Management
Trajectory Management
Operational Risk Management
Stability Management
Catastrophe Avoidance

Mission Performance Table.

With respect to the mission performance table, there are a number of factors that are important to consider. Number one is the weight as it relates to the size of the aircraft, the amount of fuel that it can carry into combat, and the amount of propulsion energy, or thrust. Thrust comes in two forms. First, it comes from the basic engine. How much thrust can a basic engine produce? Second, it comes from the afterburner. How much thrust can the engine produce when the afterburner is being utilized?

Another major component of this machine is the wing. The wing design is extremely important for all airplanes. It is part science, part art form, part experimental, and part of it is still unknown, even today. We don't know all of the elements that make up an optimum wing design for a particular set of conditions. The wing design for fighter airplanes includes such considerations as the wing sweep, aspect ratio, and camber. The key features are the wing area, leading edge devices, position of the ailerons, whether the leading edge has a straight-edge or a saw-tooth design, geometric twist, cockpit visibility, and the fuselage design with respect to its fineness ratio. More to consider is the stress capabilities—at what point does the wing become overstressed? How many Gs can it sustain? All of those things have to work together harmoniously to produce optimum wing-based performance. Those are all very important features of the machine.

What about the factors that influence air-combat performance from a human perspective? The first and foremost factor is commitment: commitment to the mission, commitment to succeed, commitment to be as good as we possibly can be. Another important factor is confidence in terms of our ability to perform well in the air-combat environment. We have to develop confidence, and it's developed over time. It's developed by having lots of flight time and experience in this arena. A third factor is being able to manage fear. Fear is a major component here because this is an extremely dangerous environment. Fear cannot be eliminated. It has to be managed because it will occur, and we have to deal with it in a constructive way.

The last factor is the cognitive system. Within the cognitive system we need certain skills. The cognitive system needs to be able to observe accurately. Observational skills don't normally come naturally; they have to be developed. They are extremely important. The second thing is we have to be able to project or we have to be able to predict a future situation from a set of current events in a very dynamic environment. So projection becomes extremely important. We have to be able to deal with unpredictability and uncertainty. We have to deal with that in some kind of meaningful way, so we have to look at things like, what is the likelihood that such-and-such will happen? What is the likelihood that this will succeed or fail? How can we set ourselves up to have a higher probability of success than the enemy that we are encountering?

We want to be able to execute whatever we think is important with precision. Precise execution of particular aspects of the maneuver, or the execution phase, is extremely important. Last but not least is that you have to be able to make good decisions. Decision making in a highly dynamic, complex environment is important and very difficult to do, but it has to be learned. It has to be part of what we bring to the fight—our ability to make correct, accurate, viable decisions. We have to be able to make those decisions in a highly dynamic, complex environment. These decisions that we make have to be based upon something other than just pure guesswork.

Decision making has to be based upon an accurate model of reality that we have constructed. This model of reality needs to be more accurate than what is being constructed by the enemy. Based upon this model of reality, we have a higher probability that our decisions will become more effective. This is so important that it has basically taken on a life of its own. It was first proposed as a major part of the ingredients for success in combat by Colonel John Boyd, US Air Force. He is one of the leading figures here and one of the Top Gun pioneers. Many think that he is the greatest strategic thinker of modern times that the United States has produced, and I would agree with that. He was quite a remarkable individual. He came up with a number of things, but I'm going to be talking about two concepts here that can help all of us understand aerial combat.

The first thing that he came up with is called the OODA Loop. It is used to define this cognitive process. OODA stands for *observe, orient, decide,* and *act.* So the first order of business is to *observe* the environment, or the battlespace. Battlespace awareness is extremely important, and it makes sure that your understanding or perception of the battlespace is in fact accurate. There are ways that you can improve your level of accuracy to improve the clarification of the battlespace, such as using an accuracy and clarification algorithm.

The second part is *orient,* or orientation. Colonel Boyd and others have pointed out that this may be the most important part of this four-step process. Orientation is extremely important. Where are you physically and conceptually? How are you positioned with respect to the enemy forces? What is your position in four dimensions? What will your position be in some future time? Orientation with respect to whatever else is going on in the airborne battlespace is vital. As a major component of that, we're looking at a particular volume of interest that the combat pilot might be interested in in the airborne battlespace as well as the maneuver space.

We have then the battlespace, volume of interest, and maneuver space. In terms of size and scope, the battlespace is the largest. The volume of interest is the second largest, and then the maneuver space is third. All of that relates to orientation—how we are orientated within each one of those spaces with respect to enemy forces. Not only from the perspective of what are the actual locations of the enemy, but what are the likely places that they could be that we don't know about. Where are they likely to be in some future point in time?

The third part of John Boyd's loop is *decide*—to make a decision in terms of this ongoing, unfolding situation. The decisions are related to what I should do now and what I should do in the future. How best can I achieve and maintain the advantage? Not to get into a particularly dangerous situation but maintain the advantage and execute the attack from an advantageous position. Not ever wanting to be on the defensive, how can I maintain the offensive? What are the key decisions that I need to make in order to achieve and maintain offense during this particular combat engagement? This has to be done in a nonlinear way because we have to continuously update our decision cycle. We have to be able to update it on a continuous basis. We also have to be able to perceive what the enemy's decision cycle is, and we have to do what John Boyd said. The way to succeed in combat is to get inside the enemy's decision cycle. To get inside the enemy's decision cycle, we anticipate and make the decisions based upon this ability to anticipate what their next move is going to be. We are always ahead of what the enemy is probably going to do.

The last item here is *action*—to act, to take action, to execute, to actually perform a particular maneuver. Notice that the maneuver phase of the air-combat engagement is done after the three other phases are considered and executed. There are a lot of cognitive activities that are going on in this complex environment of the airborne battlespace.

How can we optimize our performance in such a complex, dynamic world? That is the key. I don't know if anyone has a final solution to that question. It was kind of the big overarching problem that we were faced with as Top Gun pioneers. How do you optimize performance in a complex, hostile, dynamic, four-dimensional environment? We started out emphasizing the maneuver first and foremost, which didn't prove to be all that successful. We should have been looking at the other key features of John Boyd's OODA loop. We should have been looking at improving our observational skills and looking at this whole area called orientation. How should we orient ourselves in time and space? We should have been looking at decision making in a complex, dynamic environment. What are the decision aids that we can employ? What are the things that we should consider in terms of making better decisions than our enemy is going to make? How can we become proficient decision makers? Last, but not least, how can we learn to execute the proper maneuver that will lead to success? Ultimately, we want to succeed in combat. We want to achieve mission success. How do we do that, and how do we do that consistently when we engage the enemy? That became one of our driving parameters. It took a lot of work. I don't think we ever totally solved that problem.

I was not in any way a foremost authority on aerial combat during that period of time. I was a Top Gun pioneer along with many others. This was a time of discovery. Things were very fluid and uncertain. There were a lot of things that were on the table that were poorly understood. I discovered a number of things that were, at least from my perspective, underemphasized or not emphasized at all. First was altitude. Altitude is extremely important criteria for success, so a positive altitude metric with respect to our enemy forces was extremely important. The key element here is to maintain altitude awareness with respect to your altitude in terms of its separation vertically from the enemy forces. Second, air speed or energy state was extremely important, even vital. Maintaining a very high-energy state did a couple of things. Number one is it kept you in the fight. Number two is it enabled you to deploy agility. An aircraft that enjoys a high-energy state is almost always more agile than an aircraft that does not have a high-energy state or a superior energy state with respect to its opponent. It was extremely important to have an energy state that was superior. The third thing is that whatever fuel we had aboard the airplane had to be equal to or better than the fuel aboard the enemy aircraft. Fuel could very well be the deciding factor in any combat engagement. How much fuel is available? Another way of saying that is how much chemical energy or propulsion energy is available to you during this particular combat engagement?

That evening I completed what I thought was a fairly thorough review of these two key reports. I spent quite a bit of time studying them and trying to understand them with respect to this whole Top Gun initiative that we were going to launch the next day. This Top Gun initiative, at least with respect to my participation, involved upgrading the close-in-air combat performance capabilities of the F-4 Phantom II flight crews. The next day was our launch flight. We recognized this was a highly dangerous environment we were dealing with. We were operating an airplane at the very edge of its operating envelope, and this of course brought a lot of danger to the operation. Nevertheless, we were able to do this in a way that dramatically improved the air-combat performance of the F-4 Phantom II flight crews. I was proud to have participated in that. I was very proud as well of the determination of these F-4 Phantom II flight crews to improve their air-combat capabilities.

A US Navy McDonnell Douglas TA-4J Skyhawk (BuNo 155096) of Composite Squadron VC-13 "Saints," pictured engaging in air combat maneuvering with a McDonnell Douglas F-4S Phantom II near Marine Corps Air Station in Yuma, Arizona, in 1980.

THE AERIAL GUNFIGHTER

Oh! I have slipped the surly bonds of Earth.
—Flight Lieutenant John Magee Jr., Royal Canadian Air Force

I WAS ON DESCENT AT THE MARINE CORPS AIR STATION YUMA, IN southwestern Arizona. I was descending through 20,000 feet, and I noticed as I was viewing the landscape that the terrain was getting closer. My cruising altitude had been somewhere around 35,000 feet. We typically cruise the F-8 Crusader between 35,000 and 40,000 feet of altitude. The cruise speed was .92, which is the Mach number referencing the speed of sound. The speed of sound is Mach 1.0, so .92 is pretty close to the speed of sound. That was the cruise speed of this rather sleek and extremely fast fighter aircraft.

I had departed from the East Coast for Marine Corps Air Station Yuma for a weapons deployment along with the rest of my squadron. In military lingo we called it "Weapons Det." Basically, it's a short-term deployment to a place where we can conduct weapons training. There are not a lot of places around the United States where you can conduct weapons training. There are some weapons-training air spaces off the East Coast and the West Coast as well as in the Gulf of Mexico. This is an area of the Southwest, and this facility is called the Chocolate Mountain Gunnery Range. The Chocolate Mountains is a designated gunnery range for air-to-air and air-to-ground gunnery. I was descending into the Marine Corps Air Station Yuma and passing over the range.

We were there to engage in air-to-air gunnery training, utilizing an actual airborne target.

I hadn't been there for some time, and so I was getting reacquainted with the terrain features in the surrounding area, looking at the various landmarks that we would use in our gunnery-training practice and exercises. The detachment was probably a twelve-day duration. They usually go from about a week to about two weeks in duration.

We had to hone our combat skills in the area of air-to-air gunnery against enemy airborne targets. That required quite a bit of training and practice to get used to that environment and to get good at it. It's not an environment that would be considered easy; it's quite difficult. One of the reasons for that is the dynamic nature of this particular combat engagement—it is highly dynamic. Things are happening very rapidly. There are maneuvers that have to be considered—not only your own aircraft's maneuvers, but the enemy's aircraft maneuvers—and a whole bunch of other things that had to be calculated with a fair amount of precision.

We were engaged in this advanced airborne gunnery-training exercise because our aircraft—as were many other aircraft throughout the history of gunnery aircraft—were equipped with guns as well as missiles. Missiles were designed for a bit longer range; guns were designed specifically for close-in-air combat against near-peer adversaries. The guns we carried and the airplane that I was flying was called the F-8 Crusader. It was built by Ling-Temco-Vought (LTV). The original name of that company started out as Chance Vought, but its name changed due to certain acquisitions. That was a company that produced the Corsair during World War II, a very famous carrier-based airplane that the Navy used extensively. They designed this F-8 Crusader, a very remarkable airplane. I refer to it as the magnificent F-8 Crusader because it was a breakthrough in design in many aspects. At one time it was the fastest airplane in the world. It was the first airplane to exceed 1,000 miles an hour in straight and level flight. That equated to about Mach 1.6, which meant that the airplane had to break the sound barrier, which is not easy to do. There are a lot of things going on aerodynamically. The aerodynamic environment becomes quite turbulent and quite confusing to us humans who are not particularly equipped to understand it. Turbulent flow has to do with all kinds of things related to flow dynamics, fluids, and aerodynamics.

Breaking the sound barrier was quite an achievement. To do it in an airplane that could easily exceed the speed of sound without a lot of effort was a monumental breakthrough. This was quite an amazing airplane at the time. The F-8 Crusader received both the Collier and Thompson trophies for its incredible ability to perform things that had never been performed. It set a bunch of speed records, it was highly maneuverable, and it was a superior air-combat airplane. It was a superb Top Gun airplane. Flown by an experienced pilot, the F-8 Crusader was difficult to defeat. Most of the time it won. It was a superior performer across the board.

Why do we want to hone our skills in the area of airborne gunnery? Guns are the best way that we know of to defeat an enemy airplane in a close-in-air combat situation. The guns were the premier weapons system; in many cases they were the only weapons system that we could use. Many years later the industry came up with what they called a "dogfight missile." That was supposed to help somewhat. After lessons were learned with the F-4 Phantom II, all the fighter-type airplanes were equipped with some kind of a gun. The guns that were used in the F-8 Crusader were 20-millimeter Browning cannons. Some newer airplanes use a 50-caliber Gatling gun. A 20-millimeter is a much bigger bullet. We had four of those guns in the F-8 Crusader, and they were mounted in the nose, and they were centerline focused, which made it relatively easy to aim.

Our aiming strategy was fairly complicated. We did have some help from what is called the lead-pursuit gunsight. The lead-pursuit gunsight was originally developed in the latter years of World War II. Chuck Yeager talked about it in some of his videos that he produced for the San Diego Air & Space Museum. There may be other museums that also have recordings of Chuck Yeager talking about his exploits in World War II flying the P-51 Mustang equipped with a lead-pursuit gunsight. He claimed that the lead-pursuit gunsight improved the accuracy and the kill ratio of the Allied Forces. I have no doubt that is correct. We also had a lead-pursuit gunsight in the F-8 Crusader. It was similar to the one that was used in the P-51 Mustang. We had it in the F-11 Tiger as well, which was produced a bit earlier than the F-8 Crusader.

We had the lead-pursuit gunsight, which was going to help us to perform well in this highly dynamic environment. Because of the lessons learned, the tactics that were developed, the experiences, and the aerodynamic properties of modern jet era—all of these things came together and were producing a number of serious challenges for the operating forces. One of the challenges was to sneak up behind an airplane undetected and fire when you are straight and level—that was probably not going to happen, except in some very rare occasions. The way that a firing solution is achieved is in a turning fight. The attacking airplane is probably in a turn of some fashion. It is pulling Gs; typically, looking at the G-forces in the vicinity of about 4 Gs is a good rule of thumb. Four Gs means four times the weight of gravity. So the way to achieve a firing solution and then to fire your guns and defeat the enemy was during the firing phase, up to and including the gun-firing phase of the attack. A ballistic projectile will actually not travel in a straight line once it's launched in that environment. A ballistic projectile will have a parabolic drop to it, or a parabolic decrease, so what you had to do then is you had to lead the target, the lead pursuit. There were some gyroscopic systems developed by Elmer Sperry back in the 1930s. The Sperry gyroscope and other kinds of gyroscopic mechanisms were utilized in the lead-pursuit gunsight, which made the determination of the firing solution a bit easier for the firing phase of the combat maneuver.

There were some limitations that we had to be aware of. In the vicinity of the speed of sound, the properties of the airplane changed. The F-8 experienced these changes, although it was designed to minimize any of the abruptness in the change. Nevertheless, the aero-dynamic properties changed when you go from subsonic through the supersonic barrier and into the supersonic regime. The aerodynamic properties change, and because of that they had to be anticipated. If you are near, at, or even above the speed of sound, when you are executing this high-G maneuver, you probably are going to pass back through the sound barrier. So you're going to go from supersonic to transonic to subsonic in a fairly quick period of time. There's a significant amount of anticipation that has to be considered as you calculate the firing solution for these airborne guns. That was one of the things that we had to work on because that's a bit tricky. It's not all that straightforward. There was a lot of art along with the science that goes into something like that. That had to be actively considered.

Airborne guns date all the way back to World War I. The breakthrough there was the machine gun synchronized with the propeller of these World War I fighter airplanes. That was a huge breakthrough. Once we were able to synchronize the guns, we were able to fire the guns through the propeller arc and therefore fire the guns from a centerline position, and that improved the accuracy of the guns dramatically and enabled these airplanes to be quite effective. Airborne gunnery became a huge issue and a major contributor to success on the battlefield during World War II as well as the Korean War, the Vietnam War, and the first Gulf War.

In the long history of airborne gun fighting, we accumulated a lot of knowledge and tried to pass that down through the various communities and the various ages of the communities. There's hope among all of us that we were more successful than not in this endeavor.

So that brings us up to why we were there at the Marine Corps Air Station Yuma in southwestern Arizona. The next day was our first day on the range. We had many sorties that we flew during this weapons deployment to practice and hone our skills in this rather difficult, challenging, but extremely important area that would and does contribute to our national defense.

What's it like to fire the guns from a fighter aircraft like the F-8 Crusader? The guns we were using were the four 20-millimeter cannons. That's a lot of firepower in our possession. Typically, what we would do is we would select only two of those at a time. There were two on each side, one upper and one lower on each side of the fuselage. We would have the uppers on a switch and the lowers on another switch. The vibration was quite extraordinary. We could hear the sound was rather loud, and we could also see every fourth one was a tracer bullet. We could see the tracers going out from the airplane. The tracers were a big help. From my perspective I thought the tracer bullets were more helpful than the lead-pursuit gunsight. The lead-pursuit gunsight took a little bit of time to get used to and in some cases wasn't particularly accurate. These were early-version lead-pursuit gunsights. Since that time there have been other improvements made. One of the improvements was called an all-aspect-ratio gunsight, which improved the pursuit gunsight.

The air speed, the number of Gs we were pulling, the calculated speed, and the speed of the enemy airplane that we were engaged with—all that had to be calculated to a highly accurate degree. Combat engagement included one or more enemy airplanes. We had to figure out what their speed was. We didn't have any direct way of doing so, but we had to look at other dynamic aspects of the battlespace and figure out what the speed of the enemy airplane was to the best approximation that we could come up with in the time and space that we had. We had to do that. We had to be pretty good at it, and it took some time and practice to be able to do that. During that time, we were concentrating on our firing solution, observing the lead-pursuit gunsight, observing the tracer bullets coming out during the firing phase, feeling the Gs that we were putting on the airplane, and also figuring out how to avoid a target overshoot. The overshoot was in fact a no-man's land place to be. It could lead to a deadly collision, and so we had to avoid the overshoot. That was extremely difficult because all of these factors were coming together, and often tunnel vision was a very strong possibility. Tunnel vision would lead to an overshoot, and that would lead to catastrophe. So here's where we really worked to achieve and maintain the big picture.

I often talk about the big picture. I have a podcast called *Big Picture Thinking*. The big picture was extremely important here. We had to be able to do all of this and avoid getting tunnel vision. Probably the greatest challenge we had as fighter pilots was to learn to avoid tunnel vision. That probably was more important, probably saved more lives, and probably gave greater kill ratios or greater number of defeats of the enemy forces than anything else that I can think of. Avoidance of tunnel vision and the acquisition and the maintainability of the big picture were in fact the most important aspects of combat and the ability to achieve mission success. That's what we were dealing with here. There were a lot of things going on in this particular environment, engagement, and firing run. There were a huge number of things going on, not the least of which was the weather. What was the weather out there? Was it clear, cloudy, or windy? Were there thermals? Weather was a key factor. There were so many factors to consider: your aircraft with respect to friendly airplanes around you, enemy aircraft, support aircraft, the firing solution, the tracking, the number of Gs, the ailerons, the rudders. It all had to be fine-tuned in a way that was quite extraordinary in terms of human performance.

We were trying to figure out how to optimize performance in this highly dynamic, complex environment that we're dealing with in seconds of time. Our time horizon was very short and limited. The time for this engagement was, from start to finish, probably in the vicinity of five minutes. The firing solution where you are tracking, firing, and shooting down the enemy aircraft was less than a minute. We're looking at periods of time that could be counted in seconds. We're dealing with high time compression, so we're dealing with complex-problem solving under increased time compression. It's extremely important that we get this right, and it's extremely important that we have time to practice this and get good at it. This is what airborne combat forces were all about. This is what we tried to do to the best of our ability on a regular basis. And that's why we were at the Marine Corps Air Station Yuma on this particular spring day flying over the Chocolate Mountain Range to practice and fine-tune our combat air-to-air gunnery skills, flying the F-8 Crusader, one of the Top Gun fighters in the history of aviation.

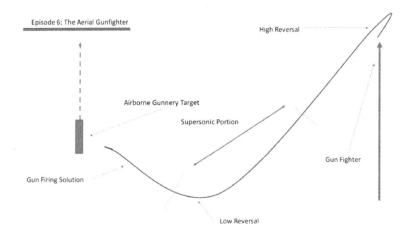

CRITICAL THINKING AND PROBLEM SOLVING
What We Can Learn from the Field of Aviation

IN A FIVE-STAR REVIEW ON AMAZON FOR MY BOOK *CRITICAL Thinking Essentials*, the reviewer mentioned something that I also mentioned in my book, which is, "The most important thing in life is not what you think but how to think."

We've talked around critical thinking and complex-problem solving, but let's go back to the beginning and consider the whole issue that is proposed by me and others—*how* to think. Are we taught or given advice on how to think? Is our formal education front-loaded with useful information on how to think? Is our continuing education focused on and front-loaded on this whole area of how to think? My answer to those questions is disappointingly no, not necessarily, and in some cases not at all. In some cases, it is done in a very limited way, and in some cases, it is done poorly.

This is something that has come a long way, and it is important for us to consider. We are going to consider critical thinking and complex-problem solving, and we're going to consider them together. Often critical thinking and complex-problem solving are treated separately. I am under the impression that they work together. Going forward, that's going to be one of my positions, my out-of-the-box thinking: critical thinking and complex-problem solving should be considered together.

There is a term called the "thinking industry." I'm using that term loosely. We can group or cluster this thinking industry into such categories as critical-thinking systems, innovation thinking, design thinking, and the list goes on. Complex-problem solving can be included; it is kind of an outlier. It's not necessarily embraced by most treatments in the area of thinking. For example, in most treatments of design thinking, they don't address themselves in any meaningful way in trying to deal with a complex design or in dealing with designing a solution to a complex problem. Designing a solution to a problem is one thing, but designing a solution to a complex problem is an entirely different ball of wax. It is seriously more challenging and more difficult. In many cases the solution is determined in some form of ad hoc reasoning. The solution is determined and implemented, but it doesn't solve the problem because it was the wrong solution, and the problem was poorly understood.

The field of aviation (like the field of air and space) and other fields like medicine present many situations in which we can experience complex problems. That's why I'm moving in this particular direction. We can see many great examples of critical thinking and complex-problem solving working together in the field of aviation. In my work in aviation, my first area was the Top Gun arena. To set the stage here, my experience was as a former squadron commander deployed aboard an aircraft carrier. It was a group of the first "super carriers" as we called them. I was aboard the USS *Constellation* when I was squadron commander. I was involved in a lot of Top Gun activities in that particular point in time and place. The second area was global commercial aviation, or long-range, oceanic operations. Those two areas are extraordinarily challenging in terms of human performance and in achieving mission success on a regular basis. That's where I come from. Critical thinking and complex-problem solving work together; they're not separate entities. Most people like to think in terms of isolated, separate entities, but reality is hardly ever like that.

It is important for us to understand how we can engage in critical thinking and complex-problem solving. We could look at it as a single package: critical thinking and complex-problem solving. These are the essential skills for mission success. The World Economic Forum has determined that complex-problem solving and critical thinking are number one and number two as the most important skill sets in the global job market today. They also point out that these are the most difficult skill sets to acquire. That's a little bit on the depressing side. Nevertheless, these are the two things that they claim will lead to personal and business success. From my perspective and my experience, I think they are correct. We should commit ourselves to dealing with that reality in an effective way.

As we prepare ourselves to dive into this intellectual area of critical thinking and complex-problem solving, we also need to look at human activity. How can we understand how humans engage the world? What are the things we do, and what is the reality that we are dealing with?

There are three categories of human activity. First, there is casual activity. You're not necessarily purposeful; it's idle time. Second, there is purposeful activity. That's something that we are doing for a purpose, and the purpose is sometimes important. Third, there is a subcategory of purposeful activities—what I call high-stakes operations. A high-stakes operation has a lot riding on the line. What we are doing or what we are attempting to do is in fact important for us, those around us, our organization, our community, our country, and even our world. What we're doing is extremely important, and success matters. Mission success is extremely urgent, it is necessary, and it is vital.

If we are going to be engaged in high-stakes operations or if we are already in high-stakes operations, then we must consider what we already have acquired in specialized training. Why do I say that? Well, what seems to be successful when we are performing under normal conditions may not lead to success under stressful conditions. There's a dividing line. Once we get into high-stakes operations, which of course is a high-stress environment, things that we thought we could do are not going to work. That's why specialized training is important.

What is critical thinking? How do I get it? Why do I need it? Here is a straightforward and simple definition: critical thinking considers all aspects of a situation so as to determine the best way forward, benefiting all concerned. There are two key ideas in this definition. It's an all-aspect or a big-picture view of the situation, and it also considers all the stakeholders. So what or who are the stakeholders in this particular case? And have we considered all aspects of this situation that can help us along the way? Critical thinking is a process by which we can open up our mind space to include all aspects. It's an all-aspect view. It could also be called big-picture thinking, a world view, or a global perspective. It considers everything. It is not piecemeal. Critical thinking is the antidote to piecemeal thinking. We either engage in piecemeal thinking or we engage in critical thinking. Those are two distinctly different ways for us to think.

Critical thinking is a discipline that began in ancient Greece. The Greek philosophers' discussions and daily lives were engaged in critical thinking. In modern times it started to become popular about thirty or forty years ago and has continued to grow in popularity. As all disciplines do, critical thinking has its own taxonomy. I have added a process model to the taxonomy to help operators and managers. Those of us who are in high-stakes operations need to have a process, steps, or a methodology for inquiry and discovery. So we have the taxonomy and the process model. There are a number of taxonomies out there that address themselves to critical thinking. Everything out there that addresses itself or at least tries to address itself to critical thinking is worthwhile and worth considering. There is the Foundation for Critical Thinking and other taxonomies out there to explore.

I'm going to briefly describe a longer taxonomy because it's worthwhile. First, there is clarity and accuracy. We want to bring clarity to a model of the situation. Critical thinking insists that we do. We want to clarify the actual, make things clear, and also be accurate in our understanding of things. In order to not go down the wrong path of discovery, we want to have some mechanisms by which we can maintain accuracy in our thinking. The second is to employ reason.

In this case it is analytic reasoning, not ad hoc reasoning. The third item is precision. We need to be precise in our language. We need to be precise in our descriptions and definitions and problem statements.

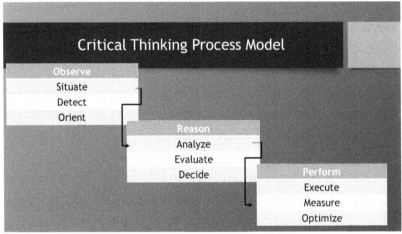

Critical Thinking Process Model

Relevance is another thing. Our thinking has to be relevant to the situation that we are involved in. We should consider things in the proper context. We often make the mistake that we consider things within the context of normality. The situation may not reside in the normal space. It may reside in an arena in which adverse conditions exist. Big-picture thinking is important here. A broader perspective gives the situation depth and breadth.

The last three items are logic, significance, and fairness. Logic certainly needs to be coherent in its approach to the situation at hand. If it's not coherent, then it is incoherent and therefore not logical. Also, how significant is this to the situation that we're dealing with? Is it of major or minor significance? Last but not least, fairness. Fairness has to do with eliminating cognitive bias. Cognitive bias is a serious human problem. Critical thinking addresses, acknowledges, and insists that if we are going to be critical thinkers, we have to be objective and fair across the board.

We want to look at critical thinking in terms of the taxonomy that we have and in terms of how we're going to employ this when we are engaged in a purposeful activity. There are three major headings here for this methodology: observe, reason, and perform. We need to observe what is going on. We need to reason about what we have observed. We need to execute and accomplish something that is productive.

The first is observe, or the observational stage. We have to make sure that we are situated in a place in which we can observe what's going on. We have to detect incoming information. A technical term here is signal detection. Then we have to orient that. Orientation is in fact an effort for us to organize our thinking into some kind of model of reality. Another term used here is mental model. We have to create some kind of a mental model of this particular situation that we find ourselves in.

The second stage is reason. Reason is in fact purposeful critical thinking. In some cases, this is referred to as higher-order reasoning, particularly when the situation becomes complex. We have to analyze, evaluate, and decide. Reasoning includes making a judgment or a decision.

Finally, since we're action-oriented, we have to perform. We have to do something, we have to execute some kind of activity, we have to measure its ongoing performance, and we have to make course corrections along the way for us to understand how things are progressing.

These are considered part of all our tool kits. We can take these tools with us on the job when we go out to try to solve some challenging and difficult problems.

There's a lot to learn about critical thinking from the field of aviation. A great reference book is *The Checklist Manifesto* by Dr. Atul Gawande. He was able to employ some solutions in aviation to solve a particularly difficult problem in medicine. Another book is *The Logic of Failure* by Dietrich Dörner. For reference purposes here are a few more books. First is the *Thinker's Guide to Analytic Thinking* by Linda Elder and Richard Paul. My book *Critical Thinking Essentials* is another good reference document, and we'll be using that quite extensively. Another book is *The Morning Mind* by Drs. Robert and Kirti Carter. That book doesn't specifically address critical thinking and complex-problem solving, but it does set the stage for improving our ability to engage in productive thought.

Aviation can inform and teach us about how to think critically, particularly in high-stress environments, and how to solve complex problems. There are some great lessons learned from aviation (and I will add air and space because we are now moving very aggressively into the space domain as well). There are many great takeaways from this human initiative. One is that we encountered a lot of unknowns in this particular arena, and we worked through these challenges. There were a lot of things that we did not know about. Aviation was new to the human condition; progress was continuous throughout the whole industry. There are a lot of things we've learned along the way. A lot of it was trial and error, but that is partly because we had never done this before, and there was not anything that we could grab onto. Many things that we were dealing with had to be in the realm of innovation and creativity. We had to solve a whole bunch of problems that deal with physics, human performance, aerodynamics, and on and on. A lot of things we just didn't know very much about.

Some of the things that we learned in the field of aviation we can apply across the board to any complex problem-solving initiative. Critical thinking and complex-problem solving are difficult things to deal with, but we could look at the field of aviation and try to understand them within the context of how they were used in that particular domain. We can look at how they were used to deal with the unknown in situations where we wanted to avoid catastrophe, in situations that we would consider to be mission critical, and in high-stakes operations.

This is a rather fascinating quote by a gentleman by the name of H. L. Mencken.[1] He said, "For every complex problem, there is an answer that is clear, simple, and wrong." That's a great takeaway because often without specialized training and without achieving a certain level of expertise, we make that mistake. We jump on a solution right away,

---

1 H. L. Mencken Quotes. BrainyQuote.com, BrainyMedia Inc, 2021. https://www.brainyquote.com/quotes/h_l_mencken_129796, accessed July 31, 2021.

not recognizing that, "Whoa, wait a minute, what is this problem that we're dealing with? Can we understand the problem better first and foremost before we jump on a solution?" That's the key here.

I've come up with another definition for complex-problem solving. Complex-problem solving involves efforts to determine the optimum solution to a performance-degrading situation while operating under conditions of complexity and uncertainty. Now here's the thing about complex-problem solving. In most of these problem-solving initiatives, I have seen many fail. Aviation is not perfect. We still make mistakes in aviation. We're trying desperately to learn from past mistakes and how to prevent mistakes from happening in the future. Our track record in this regard is actually pretty good. It's not perfect; there is no perfect world out there. We're still learning, we're still acquiring knowledge, and we're still struggling to deal with things that are extremely difficult or confusing to us.

We're dealing with three aspects of a complex problem-solving initiative. The first aspect of any complex problem-solving initiative is the problem itself. Something has occurred that has produced a performance-degrading situation that we would consider to be problematic. In other words, a problem has arisen somehow—often it is unexpected. The second aspect of any complex problem is that it is complex. We must acknowledge this reality. If we don't acknowledge this, then we are dead in the water. This is crucial. We have to be able to distinguish between a regular problem and a complex problem. We have to be able to distinguish between a problem that is either complex or not complex. If it is not a complex problem, it is a simplex problem, or a simple problem. That kind of sounds like an oxymoron, but simplex and complex are two distinctly different forms of reality. We don't have to guess. There are ways to determine whether or not a problem is complex. The third thing is, are we equipped from a mental standpoint to deal with something that is complex? If we cannot identify any kind of specialized training from the field of critical thinking and complex problem-solving, then our thinking apparatus is probably not very well equipped to deal with something that is complex.

One of the most important things for us to consider here is we need to determine whether or not we are dealing with something that is mission critical. I used the term "high-stakes operations" to mean when something is on the line. A high-stakes operation is a given, but it will become mission critical if a situation arises that will impede or degrade performance. It is very time critical that we find a solution. We must be able to find a solution quickly. It must be the correct solution to return ourselves to the proper pathways by which we can achieve mission success. So we have to be able to characterize whether or not this complex issue is also mission critical. This is vital. We cannot ignore this. It's something that we've learned in aviation. Denying or delaying a response to a mission-critical situation is a prescription for disaster. We must be decisive. We must be able to declare right away if it is mission critical. It demands our attention, and it must be solved as quickly as possible. And it must be solved correctly. There is some tolerance for errors, but it's very tight, and in some cases, there is no room for error. It must be correct, it must be perfect, it must be the optimum solution, and the execution must be performed with precision.

By definition, complex-problem solving is a nonlinear entity. That's what makes it complex. Now that we've combined it with critical thinking, I want you to consider the two together. Whenever we are going out into the world and attempting to solve a complex problem, we need to equip ourselves with the ability to think critically first and foremost and to deal with complexity effectively. Complex-problem solving requires another mental characteristic that occupies our mind space—and that is big-picture thinking, or the ability to think in terms of the big picture. Big-picture thinking is a major aspect of this challenge that we are faced with.

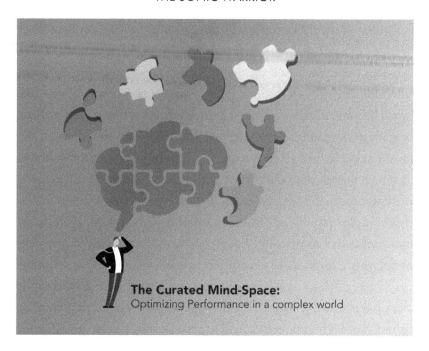

CLOSE-IN-AIR COMBAT MANEUVERING

CLOSE-IN-AIR COMBAT MANEUVERING IS ALSO REFERRED TO AS air-combat maneuvering within visual range. There are two versions of air-combat maneuvering. One of the versions is beyond visual range, and the other version is within visual range. We're going to be talking about the latter—air-combat maneuvering when you can visually see the adversary. Close-in-air combat maneuvering has been around for a very long time, almost since the beginning of aviation. It was employed in various ways during World War I—during the biplane era. It was refined somewhat by some thought leaders and leading-edge experts during the day, and then it became a major component of our air campaign during World War II. During that worldwide conflict, we had airplanes being built that were increasingly more capable of performing close-in-air combat. This included more powerful engines, better propellers, better wing design, lighter aircraft, and more fuel efficient. After that, it was employed very effectively during the Korean conflict. In particular, the F-86 being flown by the US Air Force was engaged in serious air combat against the Chinese, North Korean, and Russian Air Forces flying the MiG-15 or the MiG-17. The kill ratio for the United States Air Force during that conflict was significantly better than the adversary, and it proved the effectiveness of training of US flight crews to perform well when engaged in close-in-air combat. It also proved the effectiveness of the modern jet fighter (the F-86 primarily). The Navy version was the FJ Fury. Basically, the F-86 was the hands-down winner in being successful in close-in-air combat. It was quite a remarkable airplane. It was the last of the subsonic fighters.

It was around 1960 when the first generation of supersonic fighters was being produced in significant numbers and entering the Naval Air Force, the US Air Force, and the US Marine Corps. The US Air Force's Century Series initiatives were extremely successful. It really is the model by which we should still be building tactical airplanes. This initiative started off with the F-100 Century series. The F-100 was a supersonic aircraft. It was primarily an air-to-air aircraft, but it also had an attack role, which we also referred to as air-to-ground.

The F-101 Voodoo was not a particularly successful airplane. It did eventually morph into a role that primarily supported tactical reconnaissance, and so it performed for a while in the fleet.

The F-102 was an interceptor. It was the first true interceptor that we ever built, and the first one in the world that was designed to be an interceptor. An interceptor was not expected to perform close-in-air combat. The interceptor was primarily to be used for combat beyond visual range. The F-102 proved to be a successful airplane. Its top speed was about Mach 1.2. Mach is where the speed of sound occurs; it varies with the surrounding air temperature, so it's not a constant.

Then there was the F-104. The F-104 was designed primarily to be a point-defense interceptor. It was seriously fast and highly maneuverable. It was a Mach 2-capable airplane, so it fell into that interceptor category. It was not used very long by the US Air Force for various reasons. My guess is because the range was not long, it didn't carry a lot of gas, and it had short-duration flights. Nevertheless, it was very successful in what it was designed to do, which was to get airborne quickly, dash to the incoming bomber, and destroy the enemy-bomber formation.

Another remarkable airplane was the F-106. It was very successful. The US Air Force flew the F-106 for a very long time. It probably had thirty years of service life. It was arguably the finest interceptor. It was a Mach 2-class aircraft and very effective. It carried its weapons systems internally, and so it stayed relatively aerodynamically clean and had lower drag than other aircraft during the high-speed regime.

The Navy had two supersonic aircraft pipelines simultaneously. That occurred for various reasons, one of which was the need to have an aircraft capable of beyond-visual-range engagements, as well as visual-range engagements. That was the F-4 Phantom II for both and was a seriously supersonic airplane. It was a Mach-2-class airplane.

The other aircraft that the Navy had that was operating simultaneously with the F-4 was the F-8 Crusader. It was the first aircraft to exceed 1,000 miles per hour, so it set speed records at one time as the fastest aircraft in the world. The early versions of the F-8 Crusader were clocked at about Mach 1.6. We could put it in the category of a Mach 2-capable fighter aircraft because some versions were unofficially clocked at Mach 2.0. It was equipped differently than a lot of the other airplanes. It was equipped with guns and missiles, so it had four internally mounted 20-millimeter cannons, which made it a very formidable weapons system for close-in-air combat. It also carried sidewinder missiles. Typically, it carried two, but it was capable of carrying four sidewinder missiles. A big difference between the F-8 Crusader and all other aircraft was that nothing was carried under the wings for any purpose, including missiles or drop tanks. Drop tanks were not used during the F-8 Crusader operations because the drop tanks really didn't improve the range of the aircraft at all. It carried all of its fuel internally, it carried all of its guns internally, and the missiles that it carried were installed on special missile-carrying racks attached to the forward fuselage. So the F-8 Crusader was probably the most effective close-in-air combat aircraft that the United States ever produced. There is no official designation of such, but if you had a rating scheme or some listing of the best close-in-air combat aircraft ever built, the F-8 Crusader would certainly be high on the list. My personal opinion is that it was hands down the best close-in-air-combat aircraft that resided within the Mach 2.0 class.

The F-8 Crusader's acceleration rate far exceeded the acceleration rates of most other contemporary aircraft, and so it was extremely effective and quite a remarkable aircraft. It was an extremely agile aircraft as well. It carried all of its fuel internally, but it was a fairly long-range aircraft because the fuel load was fairly high. It had a long fuselage, so it could carry quite a bit of fuel within the fuselage.

It also had a remarkable wing. The wing design was unique during its day. The pilot had the ability to change the wing configuration from a subsonic wing to a supersonic wing by the activation of a cockpit control device. The wing designs employed on all other contemporary aircraft were compromised designs. There was no compromise with the wing design of the F-8 Crusader. It was optimized for two flight regimes. The first flight regime was subsonic flight, including maneuvering flight. It was also optimized for supersonic flight or for dash capability. If you had to employ the dash maneuver, the straight-line acceleration was crucial. It was also optimized for that. So it made the aircraft very capable. It was able to outperform most other contemporaries in the close-in-air combat environment.

What is this environment? Close-in-air combat environment is a high-G environment—G being the force of gravity. Whatever you were doing, you were pulling high Gs; these are called high-G maneuvers. We experience 1 G standing on the surface of the planet. But during accelerated maneuvers, the force of gravity increases, where we could pull up to about 6 Gs in the F-8 Crusader and the F-4 Phantom II. Since that time, in future-generation fighters, that number went up to 8 Gs. Eight Gs was pretty much beyond human capability. They were able to make some adjustments to the seat design and other things to improve the human's ability to withstand 8 Gs, but that did not prove to be completely successful. Humans were pretty much limited to about 6 Gs. That was utilizing a G-suit, which is a device that inflates and prevents blood pooling in the lower extremities.

High-G maneuvering was a major part of close-in-air combat. It took a serious toll on the body. It was very difficult. In order to do well, we had to be in great physical condition. It required the fighter pilots to engage in weightlifting. Weightlifting was an extremely important part of preparation for this environment. It also required fighter pilots to have a great deal of endurance, physical stamina, muscular strength, and mental strength. Fighter pilots had to be mentally strong. They had to be confident they could survive and that they could win in this environment. They had to be committed to winning. They were motivated primarily by mission success. They were not motivated by ego. That is a common misconception of the fighter-pilot community. Most of the fighter pilots that I knew were motivated exclusively by being able to succeed in combat and to defeat a well-trained enemy force. That was the motivation.

So we had to be tough mentally, we had to be tough physically, and we had to be well-rested. Nutrition and hydration were extremely important. We had to limit our alcoholic consumption. Again, there were quite a lot of misconceptions about the fighter-pilot community, but most of us did not consume much alcohol. That would inhibit our ability to perform well in this environment.

It was a combination of the man and machine. It was the man and machine working together to achieve something quite extraordinary. And the achievement was of course necessary. It was necessary for the defense of this country and was necessary for our survival as a nation. Air combat proved its worth during World War II. There was no question that we needed to have air-combat-capable forces always at the ready. They had to constantly engage in training practice and continuously improve.

Military pilots also had to be ready to be deployed around the world. These highly skilled elite combat forces were placed all around the world. They were also on aircraft carriers that steamed all over the world's oceans. They were at the ready. They were at the tip of the spear, and they were going to provide a safe air cover for the ground and naval forces such that they were not going to be seriously affected by enemy air power. So we were there to nullify any and all enemy air-power capabilities.

Close-in-air combat became the major area where expertise was needed, where continuous practice was required, and where our ability to engage in mission-realistic air-combat training became more and more important during the course of employing these very sophisticated weapons systems. Practicing various kinds of vertical maneuvers and acrobatics was an important part of our lives. The various acrobatic maneuvers that we could do during a solo acrobatic routine were important and essential aspects in the world of the fighter pilot. Becoming proficient at utilizing G-forces to quickly achieve directional changes for a particular aircraft was an essential skill. That was a preparatory step for close-in-air combat maneuvers.

What exactly is close-in-air combat? Close-in-air combat can be defined in a number of ways. Typically, the way we define it is by characterizing certain kinds of maneuvers. The maneuvers can be described based upon certain characteristics of the maneuvers. The known maneuvers of the day had their own name or definition. Are they the only maneuvers that could be employed in a close-in-air-combat engagement? The answer is no. But in order to understand them, we of course had to define and characterize a set of maneuvers (see Appendix A). You will hear terms like the high yo-yo, which was one of the basic close-in-air-combat maneuvers. It was effective and relatively easy to execute but required a fair amount of practice because the apex of the maneuver needed to be adjustable depending on the particular situation that you found yourself in. Then there was the lead-pursuit maneuver. That was also called a gun-firing position. That was sort of like the end game of the maneuver where you were employing a lead-pursuit type of maneuver to achieve a favorable firing position.

There were other more complicated maneuvers. There was the reverse barrel-roll maneuver, which was very popular and difficult to execute. It was a favorite maneuver that we practiced. We practiced it all the time because it utilized key aspects of a number of airplanes. Think of it as operating within a cubic space. The operational space wasn't three-dimensional, however, because it included time, making it four-dimensional. It was quite a difficult maneuver, but very effective. I considered it to be the most effective maneuver that we had in our bag of tricks. The reverse barrel roll was something that was practiced on a regular basis by all fighter pilots.

Remember, these maneuvers were intended to be executed against an adversary. So the reverse-barrel attack with respect to a similar enemy aircraft was something that was practiced on a regular basis to the extent that the fighter squadron could secure those kinds of training resources. In order to effectively train a pilot in a maneuver, the adversary aircraft had to closely resemble or be an exact airplane of enemy forces. We called it dissimilar air-combat maneuvering. Basically, the adversary aircraft had to have very close aerodynamic characteristics to the actual aircraft that we would encounter in combat conditions. This was extremely important. This was also something that over the course of the evolution of Top Gun became a sore point among fighter pilots. More and more fighter pilots were demanding that whatever adversary airplanes (we would call them Red Forces) were employed, they had to be aircraft that were very similar if not the exact airplane which would be encountered in combat. We did have, and do have, aircraft that were the exact aircraft that was, could, or would be used by the enemy air-combat forces. In many cases the Navy Fighter Weapons School was able to provide aircraft that were similar in performance to the actual enemy aircraft that we would be expected to encounter in order to succeed in conflict.

There were other maneuvers that we practiced. One was practiced on a regular basis because it was extremely dangerous. The name for the maneuver was rolling scissors. This maneuver was extremely difficult to execute, and only senior pilots or highly experienced pilots could do it well. The less experienced fighter pilots were not able to do it very well. It needed to be practiced but wasn't practiced often for various reasons. Because the aircraft were operating so close together, it was extremely dangerous to do. But it had to be recognized as a maneuver that we could very well be engaged in. We probably should have spent more time in that environment and practicing that particular maneuver, but nevertheless, there were these limitations that we had to deal with. There were some serious safety concerns that had to be acknowledged and addressed.

The last maneuver was what is typically called a loop-type of maneuver. It was also referred to as in-oblique loop. Loop is what you would expect it to be; it's a reversal of the flight path, but you reverse the direction of the aircraft by approximately 180 degrees by utilizing the vertical versus the horizontal plane. The vertical plane was very useful. Maneuvering in the vertical was not something well understood by humans. We don't think particularly well in terms of vertical thinking; we tend to think more horizontally. Fledgling pilots will make horizontal turns where experienced pilots won't. Working in the vertical became important for the fighter-pilot community in terms of understanding how to optimize the various maneuvers that we could apply during combat conditions. The vertical was the key to success. It had to be understood, employed on a regular basis, and used such that all the other maneuvers could be optimized. It was used for escape maneuvers as well. The vertical became a place where the fighter pilot resides, and he had to become comfortable with performing verti-cal-type maneuvers. That comfort zone was extremely important to achieve. Pilots could achieve it with practice, intention, and by think-ing vertically more often.

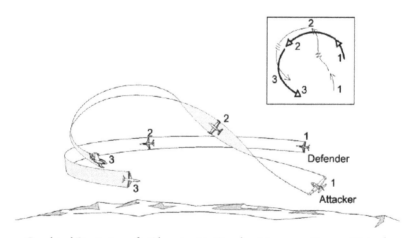

Graphical Depiction of a Close-in-Air-Combat Maneuver. Source: United States Navy–Naval Air Training Command (NAS Corpus Christi, Texas) Flight Training Instruction Manual. (Rev. 08-06 CNATRAP-821) 2006.

EPISODE 9

COMMANDING THE FIRST
Forward-Deployed Top Gun Unit

IT WAS IN THE SPRINGTIME IN THE LATE 1970S, AND WE WERE DEEPLY involved in preparing for our upcoming deployment aboard the USS *Constellation* in the Pacific theater of operation. The USS *Constellation* was a Kitty Hawk-class aircraft carrier. The *Constellation* was built and commissioned in 1963. This was one of the first of the supercarrier group. With preparations, we had a very intense operational schedule. We engaged in build-up operations with very heavy activities, long days, and lots of pressure. But it wasn't without its exciting as well as pleasurable moments, particularly when it came to feeling a sense of accomplishment.

We were going to spend two weeks at Naval Air Station Fallon, Nevada, for weapons-systems training. The Fallon Station is in the high desert of northern Nevada. There is a lot of open space and a lot of air space that has been sectioned off from any civilian traffic. There are very large military operating areas up there. It's remote and beautiful. I've been up there often and enjoy it very much.

We call weapons-systems training a Weapons Det. or Weapons Deployment. It was very intense flight operations to hone our combat skills in the area of aerial combat. I was squadron commander, so I was up there with the air wing, and we were engaged in all kinds of activities. That's when it started to dawn on many of us that we needed to think outside the box. We needed to expand our thinking and engage in some creativity and innovation. It's now being called "innovative operational concepts." I'm not even sure that term had been ever utilized up to that point, but that's what happened—we were developing some innovative operational concepts. One concept was how to defeat the modern Soviet-built surface-to-air missile systems. We were engaged in lots of practice and evaluation of how to do that. We achieved some very impressive results in that regard.

The other area that was emerging was really kind of fascinating because it was related to the F-14 community. The F-14 at that time was a brand-new weapons system. It was a new fighter that the Navy had purchased from Grumman Aerospace. It was considered to be the next-generation fighter, along with its Air Force counterpart, the F-15. The F-14 was carrier capable, and it had some rather unique features to it. It had a variable swept wing, two engines, and two vertical stabilizers. It had a crew of two—a pilot in the front seat and a weapons-systems operator in the backseat. It had very sophisticated airborne radar. Its range was about 250 miles. It carried some very sophisticated and ultra-modern air-to-air missiles and also carried a gun. It was a formidable air-combat machine.

The pilots were all fairly new to the F-14 and came from various other communities to man these squadrons. Most of the pilots came from the F-4 Phantom community, but some of them came from the F-8 Crusader community. Some of them were fresh out of the training command as well.

The idea started to generate as we learned our lesson during the Vietnam era and during the era of the F-4 Phantom. But it wasn't all that well understood. With the introduction of the F-14, there was still a consensus of opinion from headquarters and the industry that close-in-air combat was a thing of the past. Dog fighting was something for the history books.

The military industrial complex was alive and well. It was promoting its very expensive weapons systems and attributing all kinds of wonderful things associated with these expensive weapons systems. In fact, the F-14 carried a long-range air-to-air missile that was so sophisticated that it cost a million dollars apiece. Because it was so expensive, it was simply too costly to deploy such a missile in a non-combat-training environment. So the F-14 flight crews never fired this particular missile. There were other missiles aboard that were less expensive that they practiced with, and they did a great job. My favorite was the sidewinder. That was a very simple heat-seeking missile. It was the first airborne air-to-air missile. It was designed and built by Naval Air Weapons Center China Lake. It still remains, in my view, the best. It was simple, easy to carry, small, and lightweight and didn't have a lot that could go wrong. It was really quite reliable and didn't require any kind of radar guidance. It sought a heat source. It was an infrared seeker-guided airborne missile. The F-14 could carry the sidewinder, and it had a Gatling gun, and so there was a growing consensus among the flight crews actually flying that they really needed more work in the area of close-in-air combat.

Close-in-air combat was very difficult to do, and they did not believe some of the things that they had heard or were told to accept. They didn't believe that it was a thing of the past. They wanted to continue to practice—to become exceptionally good in close-in-air combat. That's what emerged from this weapons deployment at Naval Air Station Fallon. We realized we had to somehow acquire and utilize assets that would enable us to engage in mission-realistic close-in-air combat training for the F-14 squadrons that were part of Air Wing 9 and getting ready to deploy aboard the USS *Constellation* in the very near future.

Because I was flying the F-8 Crusader, assigned to Air Wing 9 and getting ready to deploy aboard the USS *Constellation* as a member of the air wing, I was approached by some folks from the F-14 community to see if we could repurpose my unit to also provide close-in-air combat training services for the F-14 community for the duration of the build-up and deployment. Was that possible? Now a little bit of explanation here. I was flying the tactical reconnaissance version of the F-8 Crusader. The Crusaders built specifically for tactical reconnaissance had similar, even improved, aerodynamic features to the fighter version. They also didn't carry anything external; there was nothing external to disrupt the airflow around the wings or the fuselage. All of these aircraft actually had received brand-new wings. That was really critical—we had to have the aircraft that was structurally sound and could withstand the environment in a very reliable way. These brand-new wings were manufactured for another version, but they were soon sent to all of the tactical reconnaissance versions of the F-8s as part of a service-life extension initiative. They had two of these initiatives going on, and this was the final one. The airplane also had upgraded engines and upgraded electrical systems. It was a formidable airplane that was extremely effective in the area of close-in-air combat. It was a fabulous platform for training the F-14 crews in close-in-air-combat operations. A properly flown F-8 Crusader was very difficult to defeat in aerial combat. It was extremely effective during the Vietnam War. It was extremely effective in Top Gun initiatives, and it was really the aircraft to engage with if you wanted to fight the best and learn how the best actually performed. The F-8 Crusader was the airplane of choice.

Working with my air wing commander, we decided to take on this challenge to repurpose my squadron to provide Top Gun services for the F-14 community. I took it on as a challenge, but also, I believed in the mission. The F-14 crews had come up with exactly what we all needed to do. They deserve a lot of credit for insisting that they receive additional training in the close-in-air-combat environment.

There were a lot of things we had to put in place in order to actually pull this off. The idea of the Top Gun initiative was centered primarily on the Navy Fighter Weapons School, which was located at Naval Air Station Miramar, San Diego, California. The Navy Fighter Weapons School was based at a major air station, and it was used to prepare crews prior to deployment. What I was doing was something entirely new. I was working with my air wing commander, being supported by the F-14 community, and taking that concept and putting it into a deployment situation. Our mission was to provide continuous training while on deployment in close-in-air combat. It required us to work closely with my air wing commander and his staff so we could secure all the necessary resources in order to make this happen. The bottom line is that this did happen and that we were successful in doing this rather unusual mission while on deployment. We provided close-in-air combat-training services for the F-14 community.

It occurred to me that if we were going to pull this additional mission off, we needed resources. We needed to look at our resource requirements. The bottom line was that we had to figure out how we could maintain a high level of operation and generate additional flight hours during the build-up and deployment of this air wing. In order to do that, we had to make sure that we had the right skill sets for our people. The human side of the equation was extremely important. We also needed to make sure that we had prepositioned aircraft replacement parts that would typically fail on a regular basis. We had to preposition those parts either in the Philippines where we would conduct port visits for replenishment and repairs or aboard the carrier. The carrier had limited space, but these larger carriers could carry more cargo.

Parts like additional engines, afterburners, wing panels, and nose landing gear were important. We had to come up with a parts list that consisted of two major categories. The first major category was insurance items. If we were going to put the aircraft in a high-stress environment, which we typically would do for air combat, we needed to recognize that some parts were going to wear out quicker. When we were running the engine at full power, the engine and the afterburner didn't last as long. So we needed additional engines, and we had them prepositioned both on the carrier and in the Philippines.

The wing was under increased stress as well. The F-8 had a rather unique wing design. The wings folded, and so there were two sections of the wings. The sections that existed outside of the wing fold were called the outer wings, and they were flexible. The outer-wing section received increased levels of stress, so we would need to preposition some of the outer-wing sections as spare parts. That was one of the insurance items.

Another part placed under extreme stress was the nose landing gear. The nose landing gear received a lot of stress during carrier arrestments, so we had to preposition additional nose landing gear struts. Those were prepositioned aboard the carrier. We also had a generator system that produced electrical power. We had additional components prepositioned, like the gyroscopic systems that were part of the roll-stabilization system for aircraft. The aircraft was fairly unstable without the roll-stabilization system working. A fighter aircraft had to be very agile. This agility meant this stability had to be relaxed. In order to provide some stabilization support, a roll-stabilization system was installed in the airplane as well. These components would wear out quicker than others and had to be prepositioned.

I came up with this idea that we needed to have a "never-out-list." A never-out-list is a list of aircraft components for which you should always have replacement spares aboard or in close proximity to your squadron spaces or to where your aircraft are being prepared and repaired when components, devices, gizmos, and gadgets fail. The airplane is always placed in very high-stress environments, and so these components will fail on a regular basis. This idea was adopted by many if not all the squadrons in the Pacific fleet.

The list was designed utilizing the 20/80 rule. We came up with the top 20 percent of the parts that we felt that we needed. The 20/80 rule is an important rule to remember and to utilize in many walks of life and activities. The top 20 percent of things produce 80 percent of the results. It's never a one-to-one relationship; it's always nonlinear. That's just the way the world works. It's been demonstrated to be true time and time again. It was discovered unexpectedly during World War II, and it has proven its worth many times over. The 20/80 rule is really important for all of us to understand and utilize in our daily existence and in our work. We had the top 20 percent of those parts located aboard the aircraft carrier. Some were also prepositioned at the Naval Air Station Cubi Point, Philippines. So we had our resources in place.

For the people side of it, we had gone out and gotten additional manpower. We were working to bring in the best talent that we could at the time. Our workforce was highly skilled. In order to develop and fine-tune our skill sets as pilots for the purposes of engaging in advanced air-combat training, we were given specialized training by designated Top Gun instructors. All of us did a crash Top Gun course to upgrade our skills, bringing them to the highest level possible so that we could perform effectively and safely. This environment was very dangerous, so safety was important, but we also needed to operate the aircraft at the limits it was capable of operating. We were also utilizing advanced and complex maneuvers that were indicative of advanced aerial combat. We were all specially trained for this new assignment.

We set out to perform this particular Top Gun-type of mission on a regular basis for the duration of the deployment. This was the first time that this was ever done. We certainly made aviation history and naval aviation history as well.

When we fast forward to the end, what exactly did we achieve? Because we had done our homework, planned meticulously, and worked diligently across the board, we were able to achieve performance levels that were considered to be extraordinary. The end result was that we provided the F-14 community and other squadrons with some very meaningful and effective advanced close-in-air combat training throughout the course of the deployment. I think that all of the F-14 pilots as well as the air wing command were very pleased that we were able to do such a thing. We were able to cover all of the requests that we had and all of our assignments without fail. We were also able to generate quite a bit more flight hours than you would typically expect for the course of the deployment. Our aircraft-readiness rate was quite exceptional. It exceeded 75 percent readiness rate through the duration of the deployment, without any major accidents or incidents. That was an extraordinary accomplishment. We also were awarded the Carrier Landing Prize for the deployment being the squadron with highest carrier-landing scores. Our achievement was exceptional for a number of reasons. First, it showed our commitment and dedication to the mission and purpose. Second, we constantly honed our skills. We constantly worked to improve in everything we did. We had very high morale in the unit throughout the course of the deployment. According to many observers, we had the highest morale of any squadron in the air wing. Everybody was very proud of being in that squadron. Everybody was very proud of what we were doing and our continuing series of accomplishments.

That was how proper human and machine resources were acquired so as to do something that was truly quite extraordinary.

Recognizing our exceptional performance, I was awarded a Citation by the Commander, US 7th Fleet.

USS *Constellation*, with CVW-9 embarked, May 1979.

DEPLOYMENT

IN THE LAST EPISODE, WE DISCUSSED THE PREPARATION PHASE—
preparing ourselves for an extended deployment in the Pacific theater
aboard the USS *Constellation*. The *Constellation* was in the Kitty
Hawk-class of super carriers. These floating flat tops were making aviation history. The manning was about five thousand humans aboard.
They could keep approximately one hundred aircraft to operate
aboard as well.

Now we want to talk about the actual deployment. In order to
discuss it, we have to understand a little bit about military operations,
the way the military is organized, how operating forces are supported,
and how they were encouraged and helped along the way as they
performed difficult tasks and activities.

An important aspect is that of command. What exactly does
the term "command" mean? The *commander* is typically referred to
as a person. A commanding officer is used to signify a person hold-
ing a certain position. Now that position is important to understand
because we're not talking necessarily about a normal organization.
We're talking about an organization that stresses leadership above
everything else. It stresses battlefield ingenuity and creativity. It
stresses innovative operational concepts and employments. It stresses
the optimization of the resources and the morale; the cohesiveness of
the organization; of everybody working together; and the elimination
of back channels, backstabbing, debilitating factors, and situations.
So command is an important thing. And once an officer reaches

that position, there are certain responsibilities and authority given. In Officer Candidate School, we learned a lot about authority and responsibility and how they work hand-in-glove—how they should be considered, how they should be dealt with, and how, as an officer, we should approach that as well. Being in command is a very important position—probably one of the most important positions that there is anywhere in the realm of the military community. It is generally recognized that the most important, most meaningful, most highly esteemed position anywhere is to be the commander of a forward-deployed combat unit. That transcends everything else in the mind of a warrior, a military person, a commissioned officer, non-commissioned officer, you name it. All other positions pale in significance within that community. They recognize the most esteemed position, and the one in which you hold the highest level of responsibility is to have command of a forward-deployed combat unit.

With that there is certain heavy responsibility. You are responsible for the well-being, the lives, the performance, and the accomplishments of your personnel. That's the way it is. That's the way we have organized ourselves; that's the way most military organizations function. The US Navy is no exception. They put a great deal of emphasis on being a commander, a commanding officer, a commanding admiral, a task force commander, and so forth.

As the commander of a forward-deployed combat unit and as the squadron commander, I had a lot of responsibility and authority. They work hand-in-glove, and they both need to be recognized. Now I realize that in some cases you could stretch the authority side of it, and you could go beyond its limits in certain cases. But one of the lessons that we learned in WWII is the value of an on-scene commander. If the on-scene commander was willing to operate outside of normal and was willing to take the initiative, he or she would be the most successful.

So I tried to live up to that when I took over this position of commander of this squadron. I tried to uphold the position and to recognize and acknowledge those who had gone before me and have been role models, who have plowed new ground where others could find direction, and who have established new pathways to success. So I looked at that, and I considered that going forward there were a bunch of things that we did that worked together. I will cover some of them to give you a kind of a flavor for what it was like out there at the tip of the spear on an aircraft carrier operating at very high tempos.

Our tempo of operations was extremely high as we went all over the Pacific theater for the duration of the deployment, including what we call the final preparation deployment. We called it "operating in the Hawaiian waters" or "the Hawaiian initiative"; it was also referred to as the "pineapple cruise." That was about a two-month span in preparing for the ultimate deployment. We had to be prepared; we had to ensure that we were capable of operating at a high level of performance and tempo. All kinds of things had to come together, including precision, accuracy, and endurance.

I flew a huge number of missions on this extended deployment. In addition to that, I worked for all of us to execute the dual mission we had. This was a new idea based upon very strong insistence from the grassroots. This was not a top-down initiative; it happened to be a bottom-up initiative. It did not originate in my area of responsibility but rather within the F-14 community. Keep in mind that the F-14 was being introduced to the fleet as a new weapons system. It was the most modern of the day. It was the most capable. The grassroots efforts that were initiated within this community I felt were to be taken very seriously, and so I did. That required a whole bunch of things to be put in place in order for that to become successful. What we were trying to do was to provide continuous, advanced, close-in-air-combat training for F-14 flight crews in Air Wing 9 deployed aboard the USS *Constellation* for the duration of the deployment. That had never ever been done before. So we had to figure out ways to make it happen. One of my primary duties as the commander of this unit was to figure out how to make it happen. Since it had never been done before, it wasn't something that was going to be easy; it was not a walk in the park. It was something that was going to be challenging, but at the same time, it was also something that was going to be rewarding. I saw that in equal measures. It was challenging but rewarding. If we could pull this off, then we would have done something quite extraordinary. And the pride that would result would be considerable. These people assigned to this squadron would be very proud of what we were able to accomplish, and the bottom line is we were proud because we were able to accomplish what we set out to do. We all did really quite well.

But a whole bunch of things had to be put in place. The first order of business was that we had to establish some kind of operating philosophy and establish certain levels of priority within the constrained resources and time frames that we had to operate in. We had to establish some kind of mechanism by which we could achieve launch-and-recovery priority. Now that's very unusual to do, and most people would consider it to be unobtainable. Most people would say it was out of bounds, we don't get to do that, or everybody has to wait their turn. There's a certain amount of logic to that, but in my defense, we were asking for this launch-and-recovery priority because this was a very demanding airplane, and the mission was extremely difficult to do. High stress and fatigue were working against us. It seemed to me that launch-and-recovery priority could reduce the risk—or at least help us manage the risk—better than if we were just one of the pack.

So we were able to achieve launch-and-recovery priority for the duration of the deployment and the buildups as well. It was not easy, but we did it. As a result, we were able to maintain adequate safety margins during the course of our operations. We achieved high operational performance rates in terms of sorties flown, flight hours, and what have you. In fact, we were able to make all of our operational commitments without fail during the course of the deployment.

If we were going to be able to perform well, we were going to need to have extra fuel available to us while airborne. Now this extra fuel we called airborne-tanker support, using the lingo of the naval aviator. Typically, we would have two tankers airborne all the time during flight operations. Some of that was for contingency purposes. We would have the low tanker orbiting about 10,000 feet and the high tanker orbiting over the ship about 15,000 to 20,000 feet. I asked for planned tanker support, and I was able to get that. That enabled us to do things that normally could not be done. The planned tanker support significantly improved our operational capabilities in our operating envelope such that we could accomplish all of the things that were required of us on a regular basis.

Priority tanking and priority launch and recovery were very important if we were going to achieve mission success for our unusual and difficult mission that we had. And we were able to do such a thing. It was quite enjoyable. I was very happy with our performance given that we asked for and were given this level of operating flexibility and a certain level of priority with respect to our access to these resources.

We had lots of support. We had additional tankers that we would utilize; we had support from the E-2 Hawkeye airborne radar system that we had available, carrier information, control CIC, and other places as well. We had strong, professional help across the board. That was very helpful to us as we were engaged in this rather difficult and critical mission.

As a quick recap, we had spare parts, we had insurance items, and we had things that were going to typically fail due to high-stress conditions that the aircraft was operating under. We used a lot of those resources, but it kept our operational readiness up and enabled us to achieve the high tempo of operations that were required during the duration of the deployment. We also talked about personnel. We had additional people aboard to help us out. Operating from a carrier is a very difficult thing to do because there were all kinds of manpower requirements with respect to safety watches and all kinds of things that had to be done aboard a modern aircraft carrier. The squadrons had to take on additional manpower burdens because of the special and unique character of carrier operations.

Also, it was important that we spend a good deal of time fine-tuning and perfecting our carrier-landing performance. Carrier landings are very difficult to do. As Barrett Tillman points out, operating from a carrier is the most difficult thing that humans have ever routinely done. I would agree with that. It required a tremendous amount of commitment, motivation, determination, and focus to develop and fine-tune our skill sets across the board. One skill set is situation awareness. Preventing tunnel vision was crucial. Situation awareness is extremely important, not only for carrier landings but in all kinds of endeavors.

Situation awareness is not typically taught. Unfortunately, we assume that humans can do it naturally and we don't need to spend much time improving its functionality. That's a convenient fiction that happens to be not true at all. We can improve our awareness of a situation by upgrading our situation-awareness skills. They are largely visual spatial as it turns out, but they are also dynamic and predictive as well.

We worked on our situational-awareness skill sets very diligently. Over the course of the weeks and months that we had been operating, we got better at being able to comprehend the situation as it was unfolding before our eyes. We got better at predicting certain things from certain current events; we were able to predict the future from a set of current events. That's a skill that we all ought to have, by the way. It's a skill that we had to develop if we were going to be safe and effective carrier pilots. Landing on a carrier is an extremely difficult and dynamic process where all kinds of things have to come together. We have to be able to project or predict the future so as to be able to respond. That whole thing became an enormous exercise in and of itself. And we had to get better; we had to be good at it. I can say this without any equivocation—all of us pilots in the squadron got particularly good at it because it was so challenging. Everybody recognized that across the board. We had the top carrier-landings scores among all of the squadrons that were deployed. We came in number one in our carrier-landing performance. We were very proud of that and rightly so. I was proud of everyone in my squadron to sustain that level of excellence throughout the duration of the deployment, which in this case was a little bit over eleven months long. That's a long time to be doing such a thing.

We were also able to upgrade the skill sets of the F-14 flight crews in the area of close-in-air combat. It had never been done before.

I think the flight crews in the F-14 community all appreciated that. They all became much better in terms of their performance, confidence level, commitment to the mission, and commitment to excellence. I saw improvements in all of their performance areas. I had a great deal of pride for these flight crews and their ability. They might have been the best fighter pilots in the world at that time. My guess is that you hear all kinds of things and hype, but from my perspective as someone who was working on the inside of this thing on a daily basis to make it not only happen but to install continuous improvement mechanisms and features made these the best fighter pilots in the world, without exception.

We were able to achieve this kind of performance while I was commanding and executing two rather unusual missions. Our first mission was repurposed to include providing close-in-air combat-training services for the F-14 community. Our second mission was to provide tactical reconnaissance. We were quite successful in both missions, and I was very proud of everyone in the organization. I'm proud that we took it on, and we rose to the challenge. We did something that had never been done before. I'm particularly proud of that and of everyone in my squadron who contributed. As a result, I was awarded a citation issued by the Commander of the 7th Fleet, Vice Admiral Robert B. Baldwin, US Navy. That was a proud moment for me. I was delighted and a bit humbled. I didn't expect it. Ultimately, the unit was given an award, the Meritorious Unit Commendation, for our performance as well.

USS *Constellation* (CV 64) en route to the Arabian Gulf to enforce no-fly zones and monitor shipping to and from Iraq. Official US Navy photograph by Airman Photographer's Mate Neil H. F. Sheinbaum (released), Pacific Ocean (April 14, 1997).

CLOSE-IN-AIR COMBAT OPERATIONS
Employing Dissimilar Types of Aircraft

THE WORLD IS COMPLEX. NO DOUBT ABOUT IT. ONE OF THE MORE complex things that humans have ever done is air-combat operations. It began during the later stages of World War I when airplanes were deployed militarily, albeit on a very limited basis. It progressed from there with improvements in aircraft performance, aerodynamics, aeronautical engineering, and avionics systems, just to name a few. There was considerable improvement across the board. This was a time for innovators to come front and center to present their new, unusual, often strange, out-of-the box ideas on how aircraft can be made to perform better, safer, and more effectively. We were always striving for a greater speed, higher altitude, and longer flight durations. Higher, faster, and longer became our model for a very long period of time.

Air combat matured into its own discipline. It was considerably helped along the way by the Top Gun initiative. My definition, which is a little different than others, is that the Top Gun initiative included not only the Navy Fighter Weapons School but the Air Force Fighter Weapons School as well. The Navy Fighter Weapons School transformed itself into the Naval Strike Warfare Center, which is located at Naval Air Station Fallon, Nevada. And the US Air Force Fighter Weapons School is still called that and is at Nellis Air Force Base right outside of Las Vegas, Nevada.

The Top Gun initiative included more than the Top Gun school, or what we call the schoolhouse. The schoolhouse was performing its responsibilities quite well. It was incorporating and embracing the art and science of close-in-air combat. Sometimes it is called visual-air combat, as opposed to beyond-visual range or longer-range air combat. So close-in-air combat is in fact a visual arena, and it is largely a human activity. There are a few things that have been developed to help a close-in-air combat mission but not very many. There is some movement afoot that is being initiated by DARPA, the Defense Advanced Research Projects Agency. They are working to see if they can come up with some additional systems-level performance aids to help the fighter pilot in the complicated close-in-air combat arena.

The problem with the close-in-air combat arena is that it's highly dynamic and complex. There are issues related to complexity and uncertainty that come into play. In some cases, there are a lot of unexpected things that happen and are very difficult to predict. Prediction is in fact very important and one of the keys to mission success, but it's very difficult to do. You have issues related to complexity and a highly dynamic, ever-changing environment. When you put those two things together, you encounter what is often called, in the area of astrophysics, a three-body problem. The three-body problem arises during the course of any air-combat engagement. We will spend some extra time on the three-body problem in Appendix B. It is described in a variety of ways, but basically, it does not have a deterministic solution. The three-body problem can only be understood in terms of probabilities, likelihoods, expectations, and anticipation. That embraces a lot of things that we could put under the category of ambiguity and uncertainty. It requires a significant amount of higher-order reasoning in order to perform well in any close-in-air combat engagement.

To prepare combat crews to perform well in a mission-realistic close-in-air combat engagement, you need an airplane that is dissimilar but replicates the enemy aircraft as closely as possible. It's important to recognize the type of aircraft the enemy is employing. You better understand its performance characteristics and the pilots flying the aircraft. You better understand their weapons systems, capabilities, and limitations. It is a very complex chessboard type of operation. There are a number of initiatives that imply this is straightforward enough that it could be programmed into some kind of intelligent technological system, like artificial intelligence, machine learning, and deep machine learning. (Mostly this is technical jargon. It really has very little meaning outside of the technical community because most people don't understand exactly what it does, what it is supposed to do, what it claims to do, and its limitations.) So we need to understand what are the limiting performance functions of an intelligent system. What are the limitations of its performance with respect to solving a complex problem—in this case to solve the three-body problem? Now remember, the three-body problem cannot be explicitly solved. It can be understood in terms of its likelihood to determine a position in space that is the most likely place that it would occur at some period of time in the future.

The F-14 community was new. The airplane was new; the flight crews were learning how to employ it effectively in a combat operation based aboard an aircraft carrier. Many of the flight crews came out of the F-4 communities; many of those were seasoned aviators. Some of the flight crews came from the training command, and this was their first combat airplane to operate as a young naval aviator. These flight crews were trying to do something unusual. The F-14 flight crews deserve a lot of credit because they were not satisfied with the way things were progressing in terms of being able to provide the necessary training for close-in-air combat operations. They began to insist on some major improvements in the way that they were trained and the way that they were expected to be trained. What they did not want first and foremost was to engage another F-14. They were not interested in that. They were more interested in dissimilar engagements, where both airplanes are not the same. During this time, the airplane had to replicate the MiG-21 because that was likely going to be the sophisticated enemy aircraft that they were expected to engage against and to succeed against in combat.

The MiG-21 was a single-seat, single-engine fighter interceptor. It was relatively small and had a long, narrow fuselage. It had a delta wing. It carried some heat-seeking missiles and some guns. We had acquired some MiG-21s, and they were being utilized in some tests and evaluations that were revealing their aerodynamic performance and air-combat capabilities with respect to engaging in air combat against a number of US aircraft currently active at the time. We had a pretty good understanding and good data about the MiG-21. Lots of interesting information was revealed. The MiG-21 was an incredible airplane if it was being piloted by a seasoned pilot. If the MiG-21 was being flown well, it was a serious adversary to be dealt with. Crews had to utilize advanced air-combat tactics and strategies and think in a way that was quicker and more effective than the enemy could. Our fighter pilots had to be able to think more critically at a faster rate than enemy pilots could think. Critical thinking became an important aspect of the game plan by which we were going to succeed in combat against a formidable enemy.

Obviously, we were not going to take the MiG-21 with us on deployment because we only had two or three, and it was not a carrier-capable aircraft. However, we did have an airplane in the US inventory that closely matched the performance capabilities of the airplane—the F-8 Crusader. The Crusader and the MiG-21 were similar in size and had similar engines, albeit the F-8 had a more powerful and more reliable engine than the MiG-21. Other performance characteristics were quite similar across the board. As it turns out, the F-8 Crusader had some significant advantages over the MiG-21 in certain flight regimes, including high-G maneuvering and high-speed dash capabilities.

I was asked to see if I could do something to help improve the close-in-air-combat fighting skills for the brand-new F-14 squadrons deployed aboard the USS *Constellation*. As previously discussed in an earlier episode, we repurposed our squadron and developed a dual mission for this particular F-8 Crusader unit, to include close-in-air-combat fighting services for the F-14 community. We did that during the course of the buildups as well as the deployment of the air wing aboard the USS *Constellation*.

The brand-new F-14 had a top speed of about Mach 2.0. It was pitted against the much older F-8 Crusader that had certain performance characteristics that still made it a formidable adversary. The F-8 had some significant performance advantages at the time. It was considered to be the premier close-in-air aircraft anywhere in the world. The F-14 needed to hold its own or succeed in combat if it were to engage an aircraft with this kind of performance capability for close-in-air combat.

So we went to work. We did a lot of performance evaluations, and we did a lot of engagements. The engagements consisted of multi-plane engagements (2v1 or 2v2 or many versus many, in the lingo of the fighter pilots) as well as single aircraft against single aircraft engagements (1v1 engagements). That's how we described these types of missions.

Because we had some concentrated time over a fairly long duration, we figured out some things that were not commonly and universally understood. We discovered the value of speed. Speed became increasingly important in our arsenal, in our bag of tricks, and in the way that we executed and performed. The ability to go fast and stay fast and to achieve extreme levels of acceleration in top-end speeds became significant when you were engaging against a different kind of an airplane. The ability to accelerate from a lower speed to a higher speed was extremely important. And that often spelled the difference between success and failure. It was extremely difficult to predict someone's future position. I like to describe it in terms of quantum theory: the more you understood the position of the target, the less you could understand its velocity. And vice versa—the more you understood its velocity, the less likely you could understand its position or location.

The critical threshold speed for encountering the uncertainty principles was about 450 knots or greater. Could you achieve speeds faster than that? Yes, for a short period of time. In close-in-air combat, where you're doing a lot of maneuvering, it was somewhat difficult, but you could probably get in the vicinity of 500 knots. If you could do such a thing, and if it made sense tactically to achieve that level of airspeed, that was good.

The other thing that we encountered was the value of the vertical. The vertical was underappreciated as we discussed in earlier episodes. We did a lot of work in the vertical. The vertical became more important than we realized for a number of reasons. Operating in the vertical is not something humans are particularly good at. Fighter pilots had to be able to improve their ability to think in the vertical. Vertical thinking became extremely important. Practicing in this arena of the vertical was one of the keys to success. If you could master the vertical better than your enemy, you were most likely going to succeed in combat. The vertical gave you lots of choices that were not necessarily available to you if you were operating in the horizontal plane. Being able to employ the vertical to your advantage was one of the higher-order skills that the fighter pilots needed to master.

You cannot achieve significant vertical displacements unless you have an excess of energy. This would require you to have sufficient air speed, which is the kinetic energy component, and enough fuel aboard so that you could employ your afterburner. Your vertical displacements should be greater (higher and faster) than what your enemy can produce. Managing energy such as kinetic energy and potential energy is extremely important. The vertical gives you the potential energy component, where the horizontal does not. So if you're fighting enemy forces in the horizontal, you do not have potential energy working for you, and you've limited yourself to only two energy components. In any kind of complex engagement, three energy components need to work together: kinetic energy, which is velocity; potential energy, which is largely altitude or the vertical displacement with respect to something; and chemical energy, or propulsion force. Chemical energy is the fuel that you have available so you can operate your engine at high power settings. That becomes important. One of the serious limitations of the MiG-21 was that it carried very little fuel. For a frontline fighter, its fuel capacity was really quite limited. But it would have had seriously degraded performance if it had been carrying fuel tanks. The way you managed your fuel was how you managed your power settings. Fuel and power were part of the energy package. Managing the energy was extremely difficult to do. Energy management became one of the keys to success. It took a lot of time and effort to train a fighter pilot in effective energy management.

The vertical could be used effectively against an airplane that employed a tighter turning radius. The vertical could also be used to reduce the visibility or to cause the adversary to lose sight of you, particularly if they were looking up skyward. It was very difficult to see airplanes from that perspective. There was no horizon reference point. So the vertical became a good place to engage or to perform advanced maneuvers against the enemy aircraft. The use of the vertical also gave us better capabilities to come up with some innovative maneuvers. Maneuver agility and maneuver effectiveness could be improved considerably.

We also learned the agility of the airplane. It was the ability of the pilot-airplane combination to change directions quickly, to alter course, and to maneuver rapidly. Another term that was often used by Colonel John Boyd was "rapid transience." It basically meant the ability to change the state of the airplane. If the airplane were in a left turn, how quickly could you alter that turn? How quickly could you reverse your turn radius to employ a right turn? How quickly could you accelerate to a higher altitude? How quickly could you turn to produce a tighter turning radius to get inside of the turning radius of the enemy airplane? Agility became an extremely valuable characteristic to employ. The ability to achieve that agility was one of the hallmarks of a proficient fighter pilot.

Close-in-air combat is very difficult. It is something that we need do if we are going to succeed in combat—and ultimately preserve our way of life. It became a very challenging, but a very important, environment in which we all needed to become proficient.

All of this close-in-air combat preparation and training was not only challenging, but it was also fraught with danger. There were all kinds of situations that would be extremely dangerous and posed a very high risk to destroying the airplane and killing the pilot. Injury from ejections was a common occurrence. That was something that was always in the back of our minds. We didn't really dwell on that very much—it came with the territory. Ejecting from an aircraft is a tricky proposition in any case, even under the best of conditions. So close-in-air combat training was extremely challenging and dangerous. We had to have certain rules of engagement in place to reduce some of the danger but not to the extent that it would do much damage to achieving the higher levels of performance that would enable us to succeed against any formidable enemy.

Advanced air-combat training employed dissimilar types of aircraft to improve the close-in-air combat skills of the F-14 community significantly. In retrospect, we were successful. This advanced-training support was very appreciated by all of the F-14 crews that I encountered. They were extremely grateful for this service we provided during the course of this carrier deployment.

An F-8E Crusader aircraft flown by Marine
fighter squadron VMF-212.

A Grumman F-14A *Tomcat* (BuNo 160391) of Fighter Squadron VF-84 *Jolly Rogers, Carrier Air Wing Eight (CVW-8)*. VF-84 flew the F-14A from 1976 until the squadron was disestablished on 01 Oct 1995. From December 1977 to July 1987, VF-84 was assigned to the aircraft carrier USS *Nimitz (CVN-68)*. The paint scheme displayed by the F-14A was typical of the 1970s.

COMPLEX-
PROBLEM SOLVING

I REMEMBER—JUST AS IF IT WERE YESTERDAY—I WAS A NAVAL AVIATOR involved in lots of flying activities. There were enormous flying opportunities. I was a department head in a fighter squadron based at Naval Air Station Oceana, located in Virginia Beach, Virginia, a major air base in a beautiful location. Virginia is a beautiful state, and Virginia Beach is especially beautiful and appealing for all of us who love the ocean, love the beach, and enjoy various water-sport activities. But something happened, and as it turns out, it was one of those major events. It was totally unexpected, although in retrospect, it probably should not have been unexpected.

We had a brand-new weapons system that we had recently purchased and deployed. It was an attempt to upgrade the air-combat capabilities of US forces. In particular, it was an attempt to upgrade the capabilities of the Naval Air Force—to introduce and deploy modern weapons systems. A modern weapons system often has relationships to advancing technology or state-of-the-art technology.

Even today, fifty years after this event occurred, we haven't quite learned the lessons. We have struggled with the meaning of this major event. We keep repeating the same mistakes over and over again, expecting to achieve different results. What I want to do here is to examine this occurrence, examine the efforts that we put in place to solve this problem, to look at it from a broader perspective, and to see if we have indeed learned our lesson from this.

What was the event? The event was the unexpectedly poor performance of our fighter crews during the early stages of the Vietnam conflict. All battle engagements have names and terms used. In World War II there was Operation Market Garden or D-Day to signify specific major battle engagements with the enemy. This was no exception. The name of this battle engagement was Rolling Thunder. The unexpected outcome was that the fighter crews both in the Navy and the Air Force were not able to perform as well as expected. Their performance was seriously defective. And I say that not to denigrate any individual or group of individuals. I have said this before—I'm going to say it again—these were the best we had, and these were great people. These were terrific pilots. They were amazing in what they could do, what they were asked to do, and how well they were able to perform.

The breakdown was a serious disconnect between the human and machine system. It was poorly designed and conceived. Now I say that with the understanding that we were as a nation, a community, a discipline, and an industry still new to designing and deploying these fast, sophisticated weapons systems. The need for speed, higher altitudes, greater range, and more lethality were crucial. We were obviously pushing the envelope, but we were also expecting certain things that should not have been expected. We were expecting the machine to do a lot more than it was actually capable of doing. The machine was seriously limited in many respects.

Whatever technology you are deploying, there are going to be certain realities that have to be recognized and have to be considered. The realities often are operational limits or operational envelopes. The realities are often the resilience of the system, the ability of the system to adapt, and how quickly the system can respond (agility). Those are the realities that were, should be, and must be understood.

In this case the realities weren't very well understood. There were lots of misconceptions about human-machine interface and lots of misunderstandings about the role of the human in the execution of this battle plan. What is the likelihood or what is the expectation with respect to the level of lethality that you bring to the battle? These were all higher-order-reasoning skill-based considerations. This higher-order reasoning was not employed very well. Things had reached a critical point. In the lingo of general-systems theory, systems science, complexity, and chaos theory, things had reached a critical state. "Critical state" means that things are falling apart, or things will quickly fall apart. They are on the verge of collapsing—you will experience catastrophe. We had reached that state. There were some serious things that had to be done quickly. So I got the call and was asked to help out.

What did the fighter community need? What was my role? To understand the problem, the F-4 Phantom II was a two-crew airplane, which was fairly new because previously, most of our fighter aircraft were single-piloted airplanes. The F-4 Phantom II had a pilot and a weapons-systems operator flying together, one behind the other. It had a significantly improved weapons system beyond anything that had flown before. But the crew was told that the system was going to do things that the system could not actually do. Things quickly started to come unglued, and I was asked to help out. I'm not sure how you could *not* respond to this challenge because people's lives were at stake. So I went to work.

Time was of the essence. We had to do something, and it had to be a crash course in close-in-air combat. That was obvious across the board. Now having said that, the devil is in the details. When you talk about advanced close-in-air-combat training, what does that entail? There are a lot of opinions out there. There is never a shortage of opinions when you encounter a serious problem or issue. As it turns out, most of the opinions were just personal opinions—they were not thoughtful, and many of them turned out to be incorrect. These opinions were not going to produce results, although those opinionated individuals with an almost unlimited supply of opinions were more than willing to express themselves.

I asked myself not what I should be *doing*, but how I should *think* about what needed to be done. What is the thinking process? What kinds of aspects of critical thinking do I need to employ before I actually decide to do something or to conduct some kind of activity?

How should I prepare myself mentally and emotionally for this serious challenge? I had some skills in the domain of critical thinking. Looking back on it, I'm not sure that I fully understood that at the time. I have met others like that, that had the same or even better skills. I began to look at this from a critical-thinking standpoint. What is it that we need to do? How can we do it? How can we get these flight crews up to speed as quickly as possible?

When we encounter a complex problem and are responsible for finding and implementing a solution, what do we do? Let's be very clear about what we mean. A complex problem is not just a run-of-the-mill problem. A complex problem exists as a separate entity and as a separate challenge. We have to understand complexity. Complexity has its own science. If you want more information about that, check out the Santa Fe Institute (www.santafe.edu) to learn much more about what it means for something to be complex.

How do we define a problem? A problem is something that is degrading performance. If there is no negative impact on the operation, then we could say that we have not yet encountered a problem. That doesn't mean that we should not be prepared for or anticipate future problems. Nevertheless, a problem is something that is degrading performance, and the overall performance is deteriorating rapidly or significantly. Things are not working as we expect them to work— in this case it could be the dynamic performance or the energy of the object. We need to find a solution and get it implemented as quickly as possible. Otherwise, we are going to face catastrophe.

A seriously degrading operational performance situation is also mission critical. In our hierarchy or in our mind-map, there are different kinds of problems. One kind of problem is complex. When we have a complex problem, there are two subcategories—either mission critical or not yet mission critical. We have to decide right away if it is mission critical. If it is mission critical, there are some things that need to be done immediately and some things we must not do at all. One of the things that we must do immediately is take decisive action. Delaying action will become disastrous. There are many reasons for this. We're not going to get into the theoretical concepts behind that assertion, but undeniably, for any mission-critical situation, we must take decisive action. Coming up with a solution and implementing it in a very short period of time is extremely important. It must be done effectively, or catastrophe will occur. We want to avoid that at all costs because it could be the total destruction of the combat units or the total destruction of the business unit.

Complex-problem solving requires us to engage our critical-thinking capabilities and our higher-order-reasoning capabilities. Critical thinking and higher-order reasoning go hand-in-glove. They're often considered to be the same thing. I would say that they are largely the same, with some emphasis that we need to step back from the literal and look at things with a big-picture perspective. Once we do that, then we are engaging higher-order reasoning. Higher-order reasoning essentially allows and enables us to think of terms in the abstract. We need to be able to go back and forth from the literal and the specific to the abstract. That should be done easily and seamlessly, but apparently, it doesn't happen very often. That's a major concern. I'm amazed at how little this is actually done by many individuals and organizations.

My efforts to train the Phantom crews could be considered complex-problem solving. I was asked to solve a very complex problem. I had to engage myself in a complex-problem solving initiative. "How to think" rather than "what to think" became my motivation. I discussed this previously in Episode 7. I quickly realized that when we are dealing with close-in-air combat, we are actually dealing with the challenge of solving a highly complex, highly dynamic problem. Essentially, the problem is to survive and to neutralize. To survive the engagement means to not get shot down. There are all kinds of ways to neutralize the lethal capabilities of the enemy forces. It could be destroying the airplane, forcing the airplane to run out of gas, or forcing the airplane to go into a cloud bank and become disoriented.

The complex problem is highly dynamic, ever changing, and exists within a four-dimensional space. The four-dimensional space is this: an x-axis, a y-axis, and a z-axis give you a cube plus time. This was discussed at length in Episode 4. The cube is being displaced along some kind of a timeline, which is the fourth dimension. The x-, y-, z-axis plus time give us four-dimensional space. To solve a problem within the context of a four-dimensional space requires a considerable amount of reimagining in our thinking process. It's not a matter of knowing the initial position and velocity of various airborne objects. What is far more important than that is to consider all aspects of this four-dimensional environment. It's all acting together in some form. We take the current position, trajectory, and velocity, and project it sometime into the future. This future projection became extremely important to do and became one of the keys to being a successful problem solver in this environment.

While dealing with complex-problem solving in a four-dimensional space, I realized a couple of things right off the bat. Number one is that where we think the airplane is going to be is not necessarily where it will be, so we have to fine-tune our ability to project. We have to accurately project a future situation from a set of current events. It's not done very well initially, but you can get pretty good at it with practice. So projection, or prediction, is an important aspect here. It's also one of the key items of the situation-awareness model developed by Dr. Mica Endsley. It's an important model I would recommend to anyone dealing with complexity. Discussions concerning complexity can be found in Episodes 5 and 7.

Something that is not very well understood in this arena is the use of the vertical. The vertical could be conceptual, actual, or a combination of the two. In this case it would be the y-axis or altitude. Altitude gives you certain things that are not available to you from the horizontal. It gives you an ability to employ potential energy (PE). The vertical is loaded with potentiality—the horizontal is not. Once you understand that the vertical gives you an additional package of PE, you begin to conceptualize innovative ways that you can employ it. There are many ways you can do that.

The ability to think vertically is important. The vertical is an important dimension not very well understood even today. I used to talk about this with the younger pilots I was training in this arena. I used to talk about swimming and how swimming could be helpful if you didn't just swim on the surface of the water but dove down into the water and came up and used the water and the vertical aspects of the water to do things with your body. We can learn a lot more about the vertical, not only from an actual standpoint but also from a conceptual standpoint.

How we connect the verticals is important as well. There is a huge connection challenge between airspeed and velocity and pulling G-forces, which are very important parts of air combat. There is an important consideration in terms of acceleration, or velocity squared ($V2$). The fuel available, the engine thrust capabilities, or power that you have at your disposal (which varies with altitude, by the way) is very important. Putting all of those things together in some kind of a coherent way that produces effective results is one of our greatest challenges. As it turns out, it's not taught very well, and it's not well understood. How we can create and maintain an optimum state considering all of those factors have not yet been figured out from an analytical or even a mathematical standpoint. I believe that there is some work going on in this area, but I don't think it has been successful yet.

In the movie trailer to *Top Gun: Maverick*, there's a line that says, "One of the finest fighter pilots this program has ever produced." That was a common phrase that was being used. To achieve that level of performance is of course highly desirable. It doesn't occur often, but when it does, we should celebrate that across the board. In critical-thinking and higher-order-reasoning terms, we're dealing with an individual, or maybe some individuals, who can handle highly complex, highly dynamic problems in a way in which they can discover and implement solutions rather quickly. They are quick, effective, and able to deal with a multitude of things simultaneously. The ability to engage in complex problem-solving initiatives becomes the key to achieving mission success. Fighter pilots have the ability to come up with a viable solution and to implement it in a very short period of time. Are they the only ones? Of course not. But they are some of the best and can do this really quite well.

It's important not to try to conjure up some kind of a solution that may or may not work. The first step in any organization ought to be, "Okay, we have a complex problem that is now considered to be mission critical. Let us call in the elite problem solvers." The elite problem solvers could come from various disciplines, like Special Forces, the air-combat arena, or Combat Aviators. They could come from areas like the medical field: ER doctors, nurses, and practitioners; first responders; and firefighters. They would form the core of the elite problem-solver communities, and they would help others get up to speed on the things that need to be done accurately, effectively, and quickly.

My desire is that all of us become better complex-problem solvers. It's the most important thing we can do as humans. Complex-problem solving is the number one sought-after skill in the job market according to the World Economic Forum. Necessarily so because it is our greatest challenge, and it's also our greatest need, not only in the business community but also in the military. We have to promote this idea of the elite problem solvers leading the way. To take this initiative across the board, elite problem solvers will initially help for the near term. The elite problem solver has considerable education, formal training, and experience in complex-problem solving. They can help others improve their complex-problem-solving capabilities as well. However, we all need to be better at our complex-problem-solving abilities.

A US Navy TA-4F Skyhawk aircraft, bottom, and an F-14 Tomcat aircraft, both assigned to Fleet Composite Squadron (VC) 13, fly together over the Pacific Ocean, near Southern California, in November 1987 (US Navy photo/released).

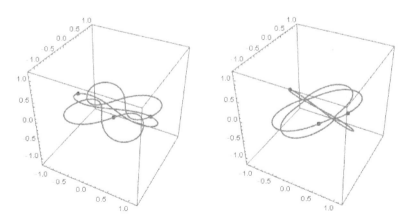

From: Jacobian of ParametricNDSolve and FindRoot for the Three-Body Problem

FIGHTER PILOT

FIGHTER PILOTS ARE A SPECIAL CLASS OF PERFORMERS, HAVING DEVEL-
oped uncommon capabilities that employ higher-order thinking.
There is not a long history of this kind of performance like there is
in other domains. It's only been around for a very short period of
time. The answer to "What is a fighter pilot?" is hard to find. Some
opinions out there will be reasonably accurate, and others will not be
at all realistic, accurate, or even close to being actual.

A fighter pilot is an action-oriented individual. A fighter pilot
loves to get out in front and take action. A fighter pilot doesn't hide
behind the bushes or hide under his desk. A fighter pilot tends to want
to be at the leading edge of thinking and action. Action is central to
the life of a fighter pilot. But there are other cognitive attributes that
we might be able to use in other areas other than aerial combat.

As we begin our exploration into the mind space of the fighter
pilot, we can uncover certain things that might prove to be bene-
ficial in other walks of life. The aviation community has provided
the medical community with some effective ways to address some of
the problems that they have in surgery. That's been documented in
The Checklist Manifesto by Dr. Atul Gawande. There have been other
cross-communication examples. We could use some of what has been
developed for aerial combat and see if it applies to other things.

I keep coming back to this central issue, a top item on anyone's
critical operational concern list—complex-problem solving. How can

we solve problems that are complex? How do we do it well and become proficient at it? Most of us will encounter problems that are complex. We should have some working knowledge of how to do it well. But the fact remains that as a group of people or professionals, we don't really know how to do it well. We don't decide up front whether or not the issue that we are facing is a problem, complex or otherwise. If the problem is complex, then it's going to require certain cognitive operations in our mind space that ordinarily would not be necessary.

What should occupy our mind space when we are engaged in a complex problem-solving initiative? There is a whole body of knowledge that supports this idea of complexity theory that we discussed in Episodes 5 and 7. We should be somewhat familiar with complexity theory and the work that is being done at the Santa Fe Institute with regard to this. We ought to be somewhat conversant in that. If we are not conversant in complexity theory, then we really need to spend a little bit of quality time getting up to speed on what complexity theory is all about.

When we encounter something that is complex, we have to deal with uncertainty. We need to deal with things that are uncertain and ambiguous because of the very nature of complexity. A complex entity is very difficult to understand because of two things: novel behavior and emergent properties. They are similar and sometimes are grouped together in a single category, but they occur more or less together. A complex entity will in fact exhibit novel behavior and will always exhibit emergent properties.

An emergent property is something that occurs at the systems level that is not detected anywhere at the component level of the system. It only occurs at the top level of the system. It's due to a number of interactions that are occurring to produce a property that somehow occurs within the overall system that is not intrinsic to any single component or any number of components of the system. An emergent property cannot be detected at the component level.

Novel behavior is similar. The actions of a complex entity are unusual, and they may not have been expected or anticipated. There may not have been a forewarning or precursor. This could be a total surprise; novel behavior is a surprise. It's also a component of Shannon's information theory, but we're not going to get into that in our discussion. A component of an information package does in fact include aspects of the element of surprise.

When we examine this whole idea of intelligently and effectively dealing with fast-moving, complex things, we start to understand the life of a fighter pilot. A fighter pilot is trained to get out in front and to take action when conditions are not totally understood. How can a fighter pilot do that? The answer is a little hard to understand because a fighter pilot lives in two dimensions simultaneously—the present and the projected place where we expect things to be in the future. T1 would be the current place in the time horizon, and T2 is some future point in the time horizon.

Living in two dimensions at once is a trained skill that is embedded in the mind space of the fighter pilot. The skill is based upon a faculty called projection. A fighter pilot can project a future situation from a set of current events. This skill can be developed. Fighter pilots are not the only ones who do such a thing. It's not the exclusive domain of aerial combat, but it is part of the reality structure for a fighter pilot.

The aspect of how to project is very poorly understood. It is not rule based; it is the ability to look at potential, expected value, probabilities, and likelihoods. What is the likelihood that this future situation will occur, given this set of events that has immediately erupted? That becomes the hallmark of a fighter pilot. This skill is very valuable in any part of the modern industrial world where things are constantly changing and are extremely dynamic. If you are involved in a large-scale dynamic system, do you need to be able to project a future situation from a set of current events? The answer is yes, you do. Okay, then how do you do it? How does a fighter pilot do that? He is projecting a future situation through time and space. He's utilizing a mental faculty called mental projection. This is done very quickly. It is fine-tuned through practice; there is a lot of time spent in practicing such a case. You could argue that you are never an expert in anything until you have ten thousand hours of practice. I would say that fighter pilots don't get that much time practicing because it is so difficult and expensive to get airborne. But the more practice you have, the better you are in this domain. Once it is fine-tuned, it becomes very accurate. It's amazing what can be done.

Any complex dynamic system will have times where things are uncertain. Heisenberg uncertainty principle is clearly in play here. Colonel John Boyd has used that in his discussions. What does it mean for something to be uncertain when we're dealing with highly dynamic systems? The more certain you are of the location of an object, element, or aspect of an agent, the less certain you are of its velocity and vice versa. The more certain you are of its velocity, the less certain you are of its position. Fighter pilots have to deal with the uncertainty principle effectively and not completely shut down.

If you're talking about the uncertainty principle and a computer system (if we embed such a thing in a computer), once the computer enters the realm of uncertainty, it shuts down. You could say because of machine learning and artificial intelligence that isn't true, and I would suggest respectfully that no, you are wrong. A computer system will not function. A computer system could be developed in the near future to project. I'm encouraging such a thing as part of the research that we should do. Nevertheless, most people, when encountering situations that are uncertain, will actually stop whatever they're doing. In the world of a fighter pilot, you can't stop. You have to continue. The airplane continues to fly. You have to get used to it and fly to the best of your ability. And you may not quite understand what is going on. Uncertainty and ambiguity have to be dealt with.

The thing that is often overlooked and completely misunderstood is that there is an analytical process that could be applied. There is such a thing as the analytics of complexity and uncertainty. There is something beyond just guesswork. There is something beyond just a knee-jerk reaction. There are ways that you can effectively deal with a given reality that is complex and uncertain. We cannot look at single components of a system one at a time and understand what the overall behavior of the system is. That gives us an idea that there may be a different way to solve problems than what we are used to. Diving into the specifics and the data may not be the correct thing to do, and it may be misleading. I suggest we consider other things before we even go down that pipeline and examine the details of the emerging situation.

A fighter pilot can't dive down to the specific details. He has to look at the big picture. The big picture is dynamic and ever changing. We need to understand the big picture in freeze frame and as it is moving through time and space. What are the dynamics and changing characteristics that we need to be aware of? What are the changing interactions between interacting components that we need to understand and deal with? What do we have to deal with and understand?

The successful and experienced fighter pilot represents a particular form of a cognitive system. A fighter pilot exhibits certain cognitive attributes that are not all that usual. Should certain people think more like a fighter pilot? How can you gain that knowledge and level of expertise? I would say yes, we should consider that certain professions and groups of experts need to think more like fighter pilots.

If we can begin to understand how to be forward-thinking, action-oriented, complex-problem solvers, we ought to be able to package it. Once we have packaged this, we can say, "This package enables you to think like a fighter pilot." We want to think like a fighter pilot because there are situations in which other kinds of thinking don't work. That's the key. First, we need to identify those areas where conventional thinking is not going to work very well. If we don't recognize that conventional thinking is not going to work, we're likely to make very serious mistakes. Second, if conventional thinking is not the way to go, then what is the alternative? Let's look at the characteristics and circumstances we are dealing with. If we're dealing with a highly dynamic system that is complex and that needs immediate attention because things are falling apart, then we need to embrace those cognitive attributes that are contained within the package of ideas that are called "think like a fighter pilot." Once we delve into those ideas and we create that mind space in our own cognitive system, then we are going to be better prepared to deal with complex-problem solving in this modern industrial world.

Time Dimension

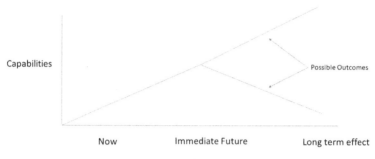

A photograph of Commander Kevin Smith while on deployment aboard the USS *Constellation* with CVW-9 in 1977, snapped by a Navy photographer.

THE STORY OF THE F-11 TIGER

MY STORY WITH THE F-11 TIGER WAS BRIEF BUT EXCITING. IT IS THE STORY of a career milestone of supersonic flight while performing aerial combat in a supersonic-capable aircraft. I first flew the F-11 Tiger in June 1965. I was stationed at the Naval Air Station Kingsville, Texas. The F-11 Tiger was part of the supersonic-training pipeline that I was going through as a student naval aviator. This aircraft was a remarkable achievement and milestone in aviation, not well understood by many folks. One of my desires in life is to point out these rather remarkable achievements in the history of aviation. I was pleased as I was going through the Smithsonian National Air and Space Museum some years ago when I saw they have an area where they celebrate this remarkable aircraft.

I flew this aircraft that was the first capable of supersonic flight. There were previous airborne supersonic vehicles, but they were entirely experimental. They were aircraft-type vehicles, but they were launched from a mothership and powered by a rocket motor. They were designed to exceed the speed of sound, which was done in 1947. The pilot that performed such a remarkable feat was Chuck Yeager. To make that distinction, the F-11 Tiger happens to be the first production aircraft that was capable of supersonic flight. It was designed to regularly achieve the speed of sound or slightly greater than the speed of sound. Its top speed was Mach 1.2, which is 1.2 times the speed of sound at 35,000 feet. The F-11 was pioneered after, and with similar aerodynamics, as the P-51 Mustang aircraft that was developed in 1940.

The Grumman F-11 Tiger is a supersonic, single-seat carrier-based United States Navy fighter aircraft in operation during the 1950s and 1960s. The F-11F was used by the Blue Angels flight team from 1957 to 1969. Grumman Aircraft Corporation made 199 Tigers, with the last aircraft being delivered to the US Navy on 23 January 1959.

As I mentioned above, the F-11 Tiger was a single-seat fighter aircraft. It had a long, narrow fuselage. Its wings were swept at 35 degrees; they were laminar-flow-design wings, which were quite thin. They were moderately long, so they had a good favorable aspect ratio with respect to supersonic flight. The laminar-flow wing has a relatively sharp leading edge. It is quite thin horizontally, not big and bulky. That gives it much smoother air flow during a very wide speed regime. This laminar-flow-wing design was probably the first wing design of its kind. It was the first aircraft to employ laminar flow with a swept-wing arrangement. It was amazingly effective in lots of ways. It had full leading-edge devices for landing. It also had full trailing-edge flaps for landing so the speed could be reduced even though the wing area was only 250 square feet. We could still get a moderately slow speed for carrier approaches.

The fuselage was also long and thin and incorporated area rule. Area rule basically means that the diameter of the fuselage was not consistent throughout. The diameter of the fuselage in the vicinity of the wings became thinner and smaller in size. This idea was first developed by aerodynamicist Richard Whitcomb. Using the area rule, they reduced the drag during the time that the aircraft was transitioning from subsonic to supersonic flight. There is an increasing drag component when the aircraft is transonic, or at the sound barrier. When an object reaches the sound barrier, the atmospheric drag caused by the air increases considerably. Once an object plane passes through the speed of sound and becomes supersonic, the drag reduces once again. So this momentary drag rise cannot be eliminated, but it can be reduced to a certain extent by refining the aerodynamic design of the airborne vehicle.

Roll control was performed by flaperons or spoilers only, and that gave the aircraft certain characteristics, favorable and unfavorable. The tail was a flying tail, which was a unit horizontal tail (UHT or unhinged tail). Being fairly small, it wasn't big enough to handle the pitch requirements for the aircraft as it was landing aboard the aircraft carrier. The airspeed had to be relatively slow. The tail wasn't big enough, but the solution wasn't to put a bigger tail on the airplane. The solution was to hinge the back area of the tail so it could act as a stabilizer but also as a hinged elevator. And so that was a rather remarkable achievement for this particular kind of aircraft, especially because it was all done mechanically. That particular tail design I'd never seen applied in any other airplane, but it was applied in this aircraft. The aircraft had a moderately powerful engine, and it had an afterburner as well.

The length of the fuselage was 45 feet, the wingspan was 31 feet, and the width of the aircraft was 27 feet. The empty weight of the airplane was 13,000 pounds, the gross weight was 21,000 pounds, and the maximum takeoff weight was 23,500 pounds. The Wright J65 engine was an afterburning turbojet engine. Its dry thrust was about 7,500 pounds, and thrust with afterburner was 10,500 pounds. So the afterburner added about 3,000 pounds to the performance. The maximum speed of the airplane was 726 miles per hour. That happened to be about Mach 1.2 at 35,000 feet. The service ceiling of the airplane was remarkably high at 49,000 feet. The rate of climb was 16,000 feet per minute. The thrust-to-weight ratio was .5. For the armament of the airplane, the Tiger had four 20 MM cannons. It was designed by Colt Industries. The Tiger also had provisions for two sidewinder missiles.

The design potential for the supersonic performance and reduced transonic drag of the F-11 Tiger stirred the interest of the US Navy. By 1953, redesigns led to a completely new aircraft by Grumman, bearing no formal resemblance to the previous Cougar. The new wing had full-span, leading-edge slats and trailing-edge flaps, with roll control achieved using spoilers only rather than traditional ailerons. Anticipating supersonic performance, the tail plane was all-moving.

That was developed as a result of testing done by Chuck Yeager. That concept was developed about 1947. The aircraft was designed for the Wright J65 turbojet. This happened to be a licensed version of the Armstrong Siddeley Sapphire engine produced by this firm in Great Britain. Now the US Navy's Bureau of Aeronautics was sufficiently impressed to order two prototypes to test. Carrier trials of the aircraft started in 1956 when the Tiger launched from and landed on the USS *Forrestal*. The F-11 Tiger was a relatively small aircraft, which was a problem because it didn't have a lot of room to carry necessary fuel, and its range was limited. But in terms of its abilities to operate from an aircraft carrier and to fly supersonically during a high-speed intercept mission, it proved effective. It was a breakthrough design; it was something that had never been done before.

How can you get an aircraft to launch from an aircraft carrier, proceed out to intercept enemy bombers near or above the speed of sound, shoot down the enemy bombers, and return to the aircraft carrier safely? That was never done before. There were many naysayers out there who were proclaiming that something like this wasn't possible. The F-11 was the first aircraft to do that, and it demonstrated that it could be done. It was not easy to do.

So what is it like to fly this aircraft? I'm going to talk about it with rather fond memories. My memories of it have never waned because flying the first supersonic aircraft was such a major milestone in my aviation career. And I began to think about it more recently when it was brought to my attention that there is an F-11 Tiger on display at the Yanks Air Museum in Chino, California. That particular aircraft is one that I actually flew when I was flying the F-11 Tiger! That airplane was my first introduction to supersonic flight and my first introduction to advanced aerial-combat training in aircraft that were capable of supersonic flight. I began my career as a Sonic Warrior in the F-11 Tiger.

This was a fascinating airplane. It was relatively straightforward, fairly predictable, and understandable. This airplane was easier to fly than other similar airplanes that I have flown. You had to be careful at high altitude, though, when trying to roll the airplane because the roll control was done entirely with spoiler-type devices. That increases the drag on one wing with respect to the other wing. You had to be quite gentle at high altitudes, otherwise the aircraft would enter a stall condition—the roll had to be coordinated with some rudder application. There had to be some rudder movement in coordination with lateral spoiler movement to help keep the aircraft in a stable condition. Pitch-wise it was quite responsive; the aircraft could do all of the vertical maneuvers. You had to watch your speed of course because it did not have a particularly powerful engine at the time, so entry speed for these maneuvers was pretty important. But from an acrobatic standpoint, it was quite good. The Blue Angels flew this remarkable airplane from 1957 to 1969. There are many YouTube videos available of the Blue Angel Flight Demonstration Team flying the F-11 Tiger. I would highly recommend them to all of the readers of this book. The F-11 did perform extremely well in the acrobatic environment because it was very agile and could change maneuvers quite quickly. I really enjoyed it because I enjoy the thrill of these kinds of maneuvers.

This thrill and enjoyment were well expressed in the movie *High Flight*, inspired by the most famous aviation poem ever written, "High Flight," by Flight Lieutenant John Gillespie Magee Jr. He expressed what I experienced in the F-11 Tiger, much more so than any other aircraft that I'd flown up to that point in time. I "have done a hundred things you have not dreamed of." I "wheeled and soared and swung high," "chased the shouting winds along," and "topped the wind-swept heights with easy grace, where neither lark, nor eagle, flew." It was amazing—an absolutely incredible experience. It was a delightful airplane to fly.

It was something that I will always cherish. I will always look back with great fondness and admiration for the engineers who built such an aircraft, for the test pilots who tested it, and for the Navy test pilots who took it through its paces and ensured that it was safe to land and take off from an aircraft carrier. All of these people deserve an enormous amount of credit. I'm not sure why they really haven't been given the credit that is due them, but there ought to be a list of all of those people somewhere that designed the airplane, tested it, and did the operational service testing of the airplane. The aircraft is on display at many museums, including the Intrepid Sea, Air & Space Museum in New York City. The following squadrons flew the F-11 in fleet operations: VF-21, VF-24, VF-33, VF-51, VF-121, VF-156, and VF-191.

Meeting of old friends: Captain Kevin Smith and an F-11 Tiger, the actual aircraft he flew, at Yanks Air Museum, Chino, California (November 2020).

CONCLUSION

Aviation is a stern master. Its lessons must be learned, or catastrophe will prevail.

In World War I, two hundred fifty aviators lost their lives in combat, while five hundred lost their lives in training accidents. In World War II, about fifteen thousand American aircraft were lost in combat, while a greater number were lost in training accidents preparing for combat. For a nation's survival and victory, domination of the airborne battlespace is vital. Indeed, without domination and control of the airborne battlespace, defeat is almost inevitable. Fortunately, these lessons have not been entirely forgotten. Yet air combat is a skill quite difficult to acquire and maintain. It is made even more difficult by an almost universal limited understanding of maneuver-warfare theory as put forward by Colonel John Boyd, US Air Force. Boyd developed the OODA Loop, which is described as *observe, orient, decide,* and *act*. Such understanding is vital.

The means by which this nation achieves air domination has been the subject of heated debate over many years, and it still goes on. In the air campaign known as Rolling Thunder, air-to-air missile technology faced its first real test. Air-to-air missiles were intended to achieve air domination without the need for any close-in-air combat engagements, negating the need for air combat maneuver proficiency. The day of the fighter pilot, it was asserted, would soon be over; the world was changing, and fighter pilots were headed for extinction. The fighter pilots' response was expressed by Tom Cruise in *Top Gun: Maverick*: "Maybe so, sir. But not today."

Advanced airborne radar and air-to-air missiles performance during the air campaign known as Rolling Thunder was abysmal. One in ten missiles actually fired, and of this number, 80 percent of these missiles went ballistic without any guidance to help them find the target. A formal study known as the *Ault Report*, named after its author Captain Frank Ault, uncovered numerous system malfunctions and discrepancies as well as inadequate training. This resulted in the birth of the "Sonic Warrior." Thus, the Sonic Warriors of the day stepped up, took over, and quickly turned around this abysmal performance.

Intellectual courage, possessed by the Sonic Warrior community, was on full display, and this book is dedicated to their efforts. I have attempted to identify some of these great warriors, but shortcomings of memory are now in play. Forgive me if I haven't mentioned all of them.

The F-14 fighter pilot community was a community I wish to single out. It was an entirely different breed, and they were the fighter pilots that I most admired. These fighter pilots rejected the rivalry that went on between the F-4 and F-8 communities, focusing instead on the best way to upgrade their skill sets against the Soviet-made and ubiquitous MiG-21. It was they who insisted on repurposing the F-8 Reconnaissance Detachment deployed aboard the USS *Constellation* to include close-in-air combat adversary training during the course of the deployment. This mission-realistic training closely duplicated the action they could expect against the MiG-21 aircraft. Consequently, the first carrier deployed Top Gun unit became a reality. This book is all about how this came about and what it means for aerial combat going forward.

I would say that my perception of aerial combat is a little bit like Gödel's incompleteness theorems. There are a lot of things that we know about this highly dynamic space where we travel at sonic speeds and where G-forces are always in play. Many times, the G-forces can exceed 6, even getting up to 8 Gs, for a short period of time. And there are a lot of things that we don't know. I would say that with respect to this environment, there are things that are known, there are things that are unknown, and there are in fact certain things that "we don't know that we don't know." Now here I am quoting Donald Rumsfeld, who was a naval aviator. There are, and there continue to be, certain things that we don't know that we don't know about aerial combat and what is the best way for us to proceed.

As we consider trans-atmospheric vehicles in the near term as well as aircraft that can achieve acceleration rates that would boggle the mind, we are struggling to try to project our knowledge base into something that can be useful in the near term and in the future. And the second thing is that we have to decide if in fact this is going to be largely a human activity, or are we going to turn it over to the machines? There have been lots of discussions as I write this book about whether or not machines can perform air combat maneuvering in some form or fashion, utilizing what is loosely defined as AI (artificial intelligence) and ML (machine learning). (Sometimes that is described as deep machine learning, whatever that means.)

The thing that I keep coming back to is that if we are going to be successful long-term and prevail against near-peer adversaries—against enemy forces that are nearly as capable as our own forces—what we need to keep in mind is that the road to success is often dependent on being *unpredictable*. Doing things that the enemy does not expect—that cannot be anticipated in any reliable way—and the ability to stay within the enemy's decision cycle is crucial for mission success. Unpredictability is crucial for our success within the airborne battlespace.

So keeping this in mind, how should we consider going forward? Are we going to invest in machine technology, or are we going to take a step back and say, "Okay, let us consider some alternative solutions." One of them is the further development of the original lightweight fighter-design concepts that was put forward by John Boyd and others. What is our mix? What are the things that we can bring into the airborne battlespace that are multi-dimensional and that are not necessarily a single platform? Maybe there are a number of platforms that we ought to be bringing into the airborne battlespace. Maybe there are certain aircraft that we have in our inventory that are optimized for certain particular aspects of the mission. Maybe having more than one type of aircraft within the battlespace, positioned in an unpredictable way, is what we should be considering as we go forward. Concerning what kinds of airborne combat systems we are going to build and how we employ such things, is there a case to be made for innovative operational employments of our forces? And so forth and so on.

This gets us into this whole discussion about what exactly do we want to achieve. How are we going to achieve such a thing? What are the human attributes that we need to stay focused upon as we go forward and as we prepare for the next air combat engagement expecting victory?

Finally, we should look at ourselves as humans having a human experience and those qualities that make humans special. Humans can create because we believe in God the Creator and draw our inspiration from such. Creation is all around us—all we need to do is notice. So let us join in and create something extraordinary.

Two US Naval Reserve Vought RF-8G Crusader aircraft from Photographic Reconnaissance Squadron 206 (VFP-206) in formation during "Reconnaissance Air Meet '86" near Bergstrom Air Force Base, Texas, on 1 November 1986, when they were the last F-8s in US Naval service. Photo by TSgt. Michael Haggerty, USAF.

TWILIGHT GATOR
By
Kevin M. Smith

Loudspeakers on the flight deck blared
"Gator on Approach."
Not a man among them doubted what this meant.
The day was long and stressful—still
They quickly took their post.
And a heartfelt prayer up to the heavens went.

The edge of night and wine-dark sea brought closure
To the day, and
Darkness descends across the eastern sky.
The reaper, indeed, might have his
Morbid way;
But tarry not—no one must idle by.

The Gator he was flying was known so
Far and wide
As the finest Gunfighter ever manned.
Such a craft brought many immense,
Enduring pride,
But was ever such a tricky bear to land.

To land the Gator safely was the
Everlasting goal,
For every Airman knew the dangers thus.
Fear of abject failure could seep into
Your very soul, so
A sturdy heart, they say, was such a must.

The deck was gently pitching as he rolled
Into the groove;
The ship had rigged for night-ops—quickly now.
Power he advanced, just a little,
Slow and smooth,
And the line-up he adjusted near the bow.

A slight settle in the middle prompts a friendly
"Power" call,
And a throttle nudge increased the engine thrust.
Pitch, the pilot adjusted, to center the
Orange meatball,
With a strong, unshaken confidence he could trust.

Line-up, again, adjusted near the looming
Landing zone,
And some power now to lock a smooth glide path.
The LSO said, "Looking good" in
Staccato monotone,
And the Gator crossed the fantail safe at last.

A cheer went up among the hands as the Gator
Caught the wire,
And rolled and stopped right on the center stripe.
The proud Gator and his pilot, at rest, can
Now retire,
For the Gator landed safe this very night.

To be a Gator pilot was a challenge to
Be met,
And those who sought this role were very few.
Such pilots, ever silent, accolades they
Seldom get.
But the Gator was the ultimate—they all knew.

*Dedicated to those daring aviators who flew the amazing F-8 Crusader,
known as the "Gator."*
Poem depicts actual events: Landing on the USS *Constellation*,
1977, South China Sea.

Captain Kevin Smith landing on the USS Constellation (1977).

FLIGHT OF THE *VALKYRIE*
By
Kevin M. Smith

The early morning takeoff was seen by
just a few,
And its powerful, hungry engines
shook the ground.
Afterburner flames expressing shades of
orange and blue,
And a shock—like rolling thunder from the sound.

The proud and awesome *Valkyrie* had left the
earth and soared,
Toward the heavens it was destined
to reside.
The soul of the machine spoke of intent
unknown before,
One could sense its unchained spirit won't subside.

This day they chanced a speed run to confirm
this thoroughbred,
And the swiftness of its form and
graceful gait.
Speed was ever building, beyond incredible
it was said,
For the Mach three barrier it will surely break.

Stunning was its speed now as the
shockwave separates,
From the sparkling delta wings
precise and true.
Contrails showed the elegance of the steadfast
path it makes;
And for the pilots: Beyond anything that they knew.

Now a champion of the wind—its kingdom the
wondrous sky;
A craft as this had finally
taken wing.
Most gaze in confused wonder, not knowing the
reason why,
For how could anyone fathom such a thing?

Undiminished was its power; unimagined was
the sight
Of the one they call the
windborne *Valkyrie.*
Many have attempted to match this
power and might;
But for others it was never meant to be.

*Dedicated to those that built, maintained, and flew
the magnificent* Valkyrie.

North American XB-70 Valkyrie (1964–1969)

Appendix A

AIR-COMBAT MANEUVERS

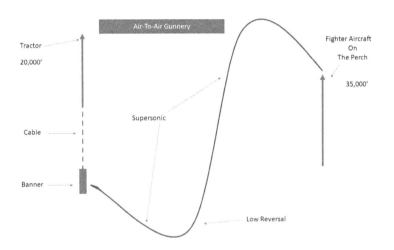

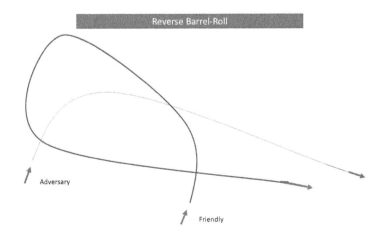

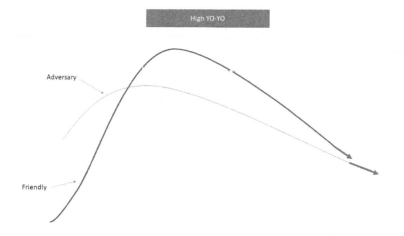

Adversary

Friendly

High YO-YO

THE THREE-
BODY PROBLEM

SONIC WARRIORS ARE OUR FIRST LINE OF DEFENSE, MAKING IT POSSI-
ble for land and sea combat forces to conduct military operations
without airborne interference. Employing combat aircraft capable of
traveling at, and above, the speed of sound, as well as maneuvering in
four-dimensional space, these fighter pilots called Sonic Warriors—
although fighter pilots are not the only Sonic Warriors since the pilots
of interceptors and bombers travel at such velocities—must be able
to operate four-dimensionally while solving a three-body problem.
It is important to realize that a three-body problem does not have a
deterministic solution, at least as far as can be determined using known
mathematical knowledge.

Solving a three-body problem is what Sonic Warriors do best,
yet surprisingly, this knowledge is available to all serious performers,
both in and out of the cockpit.

Sonic Warriors solve three-body problems utilizing the analytics
of uncertainty. The analytics of uncertainty, which replace guess work,
contain powerful tools, yet are not typically presented in traditional
curricula. I presented a number of such analytical tools to the high-tech
industry in 1988. Most of these employed out-of-the-box thinking.

Non-deterministic by nature, a three-body problem can be
understood utilizing Bayesian algorithmic reasoning where beliefs,
likelihoods, and uncertainty prevail. I would teach my Top Gun
students that the likelihood of the future position of an enemy aircraft

follows known aerodynamic parameters, and this accuracy is updated continuously using Bayesian algorithmic reasoning. In this way, guesswork is replaced by something much more accurate. While I am not going to delve into specifics here, I will say that we are dealing with nonlinear problem solving under increased time compression.

Critical thinking also comes into play.

The Sonic Warrior represents an era in which humans entered a new phase—when they could travel at supersonic speeds. While most of our attention has been on the vehicle, the human dimension is even more important yet little understood.

The key to success in any sonic operation is the ability to think critically when performing under increased time compression. Most of the knowledge we possess as humans does not consider time as an important construct. Consequently, almost all advice presented by the so-called experts proved to be wrong during this era. A new form of comprehension when complexity and uncertainty prevail—and when time compression was a stark reality—was needed. This became our greatest challenge.

Three important models of reality helped our comprehension. The first is Boyd's OODA Loop in which *observe, orient, decide,* and *act* were the cognitive processing needed for such an environment.

The second is Endsley's situation-awareness model in which projection, among other things, is specified. This model should be common knowledge among all aviation professionals.

The third is Shannon's information theory, which considers the reliable distinction between all possible alternatives. Once all possible alternatives are known, only then can effective decisions be formulated.

Taken together we begin to understand that the most important cognitive attribute when operating in the sonic realm is the ability to *project a future situation from a set of current events.* Notice that Bayesian algorithmic reasoning provides that which is necessary in this regard.

And if the situation becomes mission critical, then decisive action is required without delay.

Sonic Warriors are, above all, elite problem solvers, possessing the ability to solve even the most challenging problems when complexity and uncertainty prevail.

One of the most important considerations is the need for nonlinear problem solving under increased time compression. Formal training in this area has been slow in coming, relying on the skill of each individual Top Gun instructor. But now it is time to create a formal curriculum that effectively teaches this important subject—not just to aviators.

The most important feature of any Sonic Warrior-type training is Colonel John Boyd's OODA Loop. Hopefully, this is being taught in all basic and advanced flight curriculums.

- Observe: Observation skills need to be developed. Observation and visualization enhancement initiatives should be made available.
- Orientation: The ability to orient oneself within a dynamic model of reality is essential. Building such a dynamic model is enormously difficult yet essential for mission success.
- Decide: Operational decision making is without question essential for mission success. Here such a model as that presented by Smith and Larrieu can be most useful, as found in *Mission Adaptive Display Technologies and Operational Decision Making in Aviation*.
- Act: To act decisively, while executing needed activities with precision, is important as well. Here precision maneuver guidance should be a key feature of the human-machine system. The human aspects of a Sonic Warrior reveal that intuition, innovation, and creativity are vital for mission success as well.

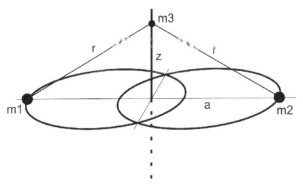

An Illustration of the Three-Body Problem *

A US Marine Corps McDonnell Douglas F/A-18A *Hornet* of Marine Fighter Attack Training Squadron VMFAT-101 engages in air-combat maneuvering with IAI F-21A *Kfir* and Northrop F-5E *Tiger II* aggressor aircraft in the skies near Marine Corps Air Station, Yuma, Arizona, in 1989.

NO PLACE I'D RATHER BE

by Rob Rivers

No place I'd rather be. That has become an ethos for me over the years as I found myself gaining more and more appreciation for my life with each passing year. Even doing my taxes, I can honestly say— well, almost honestly—that there is no place I would rather be. If I'm working on my income tax return, it means I made some money, and if I made some money, it was most likely from doing something that I loved. "No place I'd rather be" came for me from learning to fly in college. There was no place I would rather be than in an airplane. That sentiment took a huge leap when I became a naval aviator, though I had not, even then, put words to that feeling. Those years gave way to becoming an airline pilot, to owning my own airplanes, to becoming a NASA test pilot, and finally, to becoming a contract test pilot. All along I flew general aviation airplanes, and for the past forty years, my own airplanes on the side. It was several years ago when flying one of my planes back from a business trip to Florida, once again having the time of my life while studying the Georgia Barrier Islands from 1,000 feet, that those words came to me: there was truly no place I would rather be than in my airplane at that moment.

Like all lives, mine has had its ups and downs. The downs—a broken heart, death of family and friends, setbacks at work—were for me, fortunately, dwarfed by the ups—falling in love, having children, success at work. When I contemplate why I have had such a blessed life despite the occasional pain, the one thread throughout that kept me

175

always optimistic and happy was flying. Whenever the blues caught up to me, I would go fly. Whenever I felt on top of the world, I would go fly. I took my sons flying with me when they were each only eighteen months old, and we have flown together ever since. My family and I took many trips together in our family airplane. My oldest son will soon be leaving for flight school to become a naval aviator like me. My youngest son is now thinking of doing the same. I think they saw in me the joy of that profession.

For me, being a naval aviator set the pattern for my life, indelibly etching within me perpetual youth and excitement. It changed forever how I saw the world and how I came to behave in the world. I learned that life is precious, that it can end in seconds, that Death leaps out of nowhere when least expected. Life must therefore be lived to the fullest, never giving in to a fear of death. I learned never to take myself too seriously since just when I thought I had it all figured out, I boltered. I learned that there will always be someone better but to never stop trying to be the best. I learned the values of courage, loyalty, teamwork, and honor. Most importantly, I learned that life can be pure joy. When learning to fly the F-8 Crusader as a newly minted naval aviator, my fellow students and I believed in the Law of Conservation of Fun. That law states, more or less, that in the entire universe fun remains constant. Like mass, it can neither be created nor destroyed. If fun decreases somewhere in the universe, it must increase somewhere else. We believed that we were flying F-8s to help maintain the balance of fun in the universe. With all of the wars and pestilence and personal losses, fun was always decreasing and always under attack. It was up to us to keep the balance by having more fun than humanly possible. And did we have fun!

Imagine turning a brand-new naval aviator—full of spit and vinegar, hair on fire with a feeling of immortality—loose with the most remarkable jet fighter ever built! From mock dogfights with other young pilots (whose hair burned just as brightly), to flying on the desert floor at cactus level at almost 600 miles per hour, to seeing the reflection in Crater Lake that made it impossible to tell where the land ended and the water began, to seeing God's most perfect sunset in the west and brilliant, perfectly circular rainbows in the east and not being able to fly in circles fast enough to see them enough—these experiences are gloriously seared in my memory. Being launched by a catapult from an aircraft carrier into the deepest blue sky you can imagine in a matter of seconds and then flying a mission over the middle of the Pacific Ocean, finding the carrier two hours later, being first into the break north of 500 knots, breaking at the bow, getting the gear down on the downwind, and grabbing a three-wire left you with a feeling of such fulfillment and confidence that you could not imagine *not* succeeding at anything to which you set your mind.

There was, indeed, no place I'd rather be back in the days of flying an F-8 Crusader aboard ship. The truly wondrous miracle is that to this day there is still no place I'd rather be. The naval aviator will never leave me.

APPENDIX D

ADDITIONAL READING
AND KEY PLAYERS

Additional Reading

Carter, Kirti and Robert Carter. *The Morning Mind: Use Your Brain to Master Your Day and Supercharge Your Life*. New York: AMACOM, 2019.

Coram, Robert. *Boyd: The Fighter Pilot Who Changed the Art of War*. New York: Hachette Book Group, 2002.

Defense Intelligence Agency. Declassified on March 23, 2000. *Have Doughnut (U): Tactical*. Accessed on December 30, 2020. https://nsarchive2.gwu.edu//NSAEBB/NSAEBB443/docs/area51_50.PDF.

Dörner, Dietrich. *The Logic of Failure: Recognizing and Avoiding Error in Complex Situations*. New York: Basic Books, 2009.

Elder, Linda and Richard Paul. *Thinker's Guide to Analytic Thinking: How to Take Thinking Apart and What to Look for When You Do*. Washington, DC: Rowman & Littlefield, 2016.

Gawande, Atul. *The Checklist Manifesto: How to Get Things Right*. New York: Metropolitan Books, 2009. New York: Penguin, 2014.

Hampton, Dan. *Lords of the Sky: Fighter Pilots and Air Combat, from the Red Baron to the F-16*. New York: William Morrow Paperbacks, 2015.

Hurt Jr., Harry. H. *Aerodynamics for Naval Aviators*. Los Angeles: University of Southern California, 1965.

Lohrenz, Carey D. *Fearless Leadership: High-Performance Lessons from the Flight Deck*. Austin: Greenleaf Book Group, 2012.

Mencken, H. L. *H. L. Mencken Quotes*. BrainyQuote.com, BrainyMedia Inc, 2021. https://www.brainyquote.com/quotes/ h_l_mencken_129796, accessed July 31, 2021.

Mersky, Peter. *Vought F-8 Crusader*. United Kingdom: Osprey Publishing Ltd., 1989.

Naval History and Heritage Command. *Report of the Air-to-Air Missile System Capability Review, July–November 1968* (a.k.a. *The Ault Report*). Accessed on December 30, 2020. https:// www.history.navy.mil/research/histories/naval-aviation-history/ ault-report.html.

Olds, Christina, Robin Olds, and Ed Rasimus. *Fighter Pilot*. New York: Saint Martin's Publishing Group, 2010.

Pedersen, Dan. *Topgun: An American Story*. New York: Hachette Books, 2019.

Sayers, William. "The Red Baron Reports: What They Really Said." *Air Power History* 52(3) 4–13. Accessed on December 30, 2020. https://www.afhistory.org/wp-content/uploads/2005_fall.pdf.

Shaw, Robert L. *Fighter Combat: Tactics and Maneuvering*. Annapolis: Naval Institute Press, 1985.

Smith, Kevin M., and Stephane Larrieu. *Mission Adaptive Display Technologies and Operational Decision Making in Aviation*. Hershey: IGI-Global, 2015.

Smith, Kevin M. *Critical Thinking Essentials*. La Vergne: IngramSpark, 2016.

Smith, Kevin M. "Decision Making in Complex Environments." *International Journal of Aviation Systems, Operations, and Training* (IJASOT). Hershey: IGI-Global, 2019.

Snodgrass, Guy M. *Topgun's Top 10: Leadership Lessons from the Cockpit*. New York: Center Street, 2020.

Wikipedia. "VFC-13." Accessed on January 5, 2021. https://en.wiki-pedia.org/wiki/VFC-13.

Wikipedia. "VFC-111." Accessed on January 22, 2021. https://en.wikipedia.org/wiki/VFC-111.

Key Players

- Captain Frank Ault, USN, author of the *Ault Report*
- Commander David M. Beam, USN, Last Commander, VFP-63
- Colonel John Boyd, USAF, developed the maneuver-warfare theory and the power equation
- Captain "Bill" Kiper, USN, former commander VF-302, *Have Doughnut* principal investigator
- Vice Admiral Anthony "Tony" Less, USN, former air wing commander (CVW-9), USS *Constellation*, US 7th Fleet; former commander, Blue Angels
- Lieutenant "Marty" Martin, USN, VFP-63 (RIP)
- Brigadier General Robin Olds, USAF, nation's greatest fighter pilot
- Captain Dan Pedersen, USN, founder of Top Gun
- Lieutenant Chuck Potter, USN, VFP-63 (RIP)
- Commander "Rob" Rivers, USN, VFP-63, USS *Constellation*
- Brigadier General Chuck Yeager, USAF, first Sonic Warrior

ORDER INFORMATION

REDEMPTION
PRESS

To order additional copies of this book, please visit
www.redemption-press.com.
Also available on Amazon.com and BarnesandNoble.com
or by calling toll-free 1-844-2REDEEM.

CPSIA information can be obtained
at www.ICGtesting.com
Printed in the USA
BVHW052307090223
658261BV00015B/150/J

9 781646 455003